LONGBOWS IN THE FAR NORTH

LONGBOWS IN THE FAR NORTH

An Archer's Adventures in Alaska and Siberia

E. DONNALL THOMAS, JR.

STACKPOLE
BOOKS

Published by
STACKPOLE BOOKS
5067 Ritter Road
Mechanicsburg, PA 17055

Printed in the United States of America

10 9 8 7 6 5 4

First Edition

A NUMBER OF the chapters in this book have appeared in print previously. The original
versions of "A Bull from the Burn," "The Prize," "Bows, Arrows, and Dangerous Game,"
"Russian Bears, Part 1: Close Encounters," "Bear Country," "Tundra Journal," and
"Desperately Seeking Alaska" appeared in *Bowhunter Magazine.* "The Stalk" appeared in
Game Country. "Zen in the Art of Bear Hunting" appeared in the 1990 issue of *Professional
Bowhunter Annual.* "Kid Stuff" and "Ashes to Ashes" were published in *Traditional
Bowhunter.* "Russian Bears, Part 2: And Nothing But the Truth" appeared in *Gray's Sporting
Journal.* "Thank You, Sensei" was published in *Game Journal.*

Library of Congress Cataloging-in-Publication Data

Thomas, E. Donnall.
    Longbows in the far north : an archer's adventures in Alaska and
Siberia / E. Donall Thomas, Jr. — 1st ed.
        p.   cm.
    ISBN 0-8117-0956-6
    1. Thomas, E. Donnall.   2. Bowhunting—Alaska.   3. Bowhunting—
Russia (Federation)—Siberia.   4. Big game hunting—Alaska.   5. Big
game hunting—Russia (Federation)—Siberia.   6. Archers—United
States—Biography.   I. Title.
SK36.T48   1993
799.2'6'09798—dc20   93-3148
                                                                        CIP

For my mother and father,
who first introduced me to the joy of wild places.

CONTENTS

ACKNOWLEDGMENTS

THE BUSINESS OF outdoor writing can be frustrating, especially for those who insist on defying proven formulas and taking chances with new ways of examining the natural world around them. At the risk of an omission I may later regret, I would like to thank the following writers and editors for encouraging me to write about bowhunting my own way: John Barsness, Dave Canfield, Wade Carstens, Jim Chinn, Eileen Clarke, Tim Conrads, David Foster, John Hewitt, M. R. James, Jay Massey, Jack Smith, David Wonderlich, and of course, Judith Schnell of Stackpole Books.

PREFACE

HUNTING IS FACING its time of crisis in our culture. Outdoor writers (a term I dislike but continue to use for want of an alternative) have not always served our cause well. This is particularly true of writing about bowhunting, which all too often descends into catalogs of record book scores and personal accomplishment, thereby missing most of the point.

For the fact remains that the central step in becoming a bowhunter is the conscious decision to limit one's means of take in the field. Once this decision is made, it is clear that most hunts will end without anything being taken in the conventional sense. The sixteen stories and essays in this collection reflect this fact. Some readers will decry a number of these hunts as "unsuccessful." That is their privilege. That is also their problem.

One of the difficulties facing outdoor writers (that term again!) is the tacit need for so many of us to present ourselves as experts. It is my impression that the ability to hunt well and the ability to write well are randomly correlated at best. In this regard, I want to be quite candid from the start. I do not consider myself a particularly good bowhunter. I lose a great many contests in the field, and not just because I have chosen to stack the deck in my quarry's favor by severely limiting my equipment. While I have enjoyed a measure of success, that success is the product of two simple factors (in addition to the omnipresent element of luck). Because I love the outdoors, I spend a lot of time there, and in the art of bowhunting there is no substitute for patience. A lifelong fascination with wildlife has given me a better than average knowledge of my quarry. That's it; there are no other secrets, and the reader in search of magical ways to increase his or her harvest with the bow should be advised to look elsewhere. I don't know any, and if I did I probably wouldn't tell you about them.

The focus of this collection of bowhunting stories is the Far North, specifically Alaska, where I lived for several years, and the former Soviet Far East, whose reaches I was fortunate enough to be one of the first American bowhunters to explore. I chose this locale because the country and people are intrinsically fascinating, even to readers with little knowledge of the bow. While two of the chapters (on bear attacks and practical aspects of bowhunting in Alaska) do contain conventionally useful information, I confess to being far more interested in the why than the how of all of this.

I hope that by the end of the last chapter you will be, too.

ONE

The Stalk

I WAS FAMILIAR enough with the country to know that we would soon be hiking through a stunning expanse of open tundra, but there was no way for my senses to confirm my expectations. We had crawled out of our tents an hour earlier to find the spruce trees dripping and the Mulchatna Valley enveloped in the dense fog that typically follows the passage of a late summer frontal system through southwestern Alaska. With visibility limited to thirty yards, hunting seemed futile. This would have been a fine morning to get on with the float trip and fish our way down another dozen miles of river. We couldn't afford a leisurely day with the fly rods, however. The previous afternoon, Montana bowhunter Dick LeBlond had slipped a cedar shaft behind the shoulder of a trophy-class caribou in the hills behind our camp, and now a hard day of packing lay ahead of us.

Dick shouldered my camp rifle, the .375 that I no longer used for any purpose other than bear security. Packing fresh caribou hindquarters through the heart of grizzly country would certainly justify its presence that day. Ray Stalmaster and I strung our bows and touched up a few broadheads. You never know when you might need a sharp one.

As a matter of simple aesthetics, the two most exotic big game animals in North America, for my money, are the pronghorn and the caribou. On a continent whose ungulates are expected to dress in basic brown, the striking color schemes these two species sport serve immediate notice that the observer is on to something special. After spending most of my adult life in Montana and Alaska, I have glassed and studied countless thousands of each, but they still don't seem ordinary. I hope they never do.

The caribou population of North America consists of several widely dispersed subspecies, of which five are acknowledged as distinct for sporting classification purposes: woodland, mountain, Quebec-Labrador, barren ground, and the newly recognized Perry caribou of the central Canadian Arctic plain. They are all *Rangifer tarandus,* the biologists tell us, although the trained eye can often distinguish the antlers of some varieties at a glance—for example, the bottom-heavy, flat-bladed racks of the woodland subspecies or the club-topped main beams of a specimen from northern Quebec. Most of the lot are Canadian citizens. While the caribou's historic range included the northeastern United States, and mountain caribou still occasionally wander into parts of Idaho and Washington, caribou hunting in our country practically means hunting Alaska for barren ground bulls, *Rangifer tarandus grantii.*

With the possible exception of the black bear, the caribou is Alaska's most widely distributed big game species. Caribou are found in huntable numbers in almost all of Alaska's twenty-six game management units except those of the southeastern panhandle. Alaska's caribou form a dozen or so more or less distinct populations, ranging in size from the hundreds of thousands of animals in the western Arctic to the small, carefully managed herds of the Kenai Peninsula. While I have pursued caribou with the bow from one end of the state to the other, it is the Mulchatna herd inhabiting the western slope of the Alaska Range and its adjacent foothills that has always seemed to offer caribou hunting in its truest form. This was the country that my Montana visitors and I were floating through now.

Dick's fallen bull lay field dressed five miles and one drainage away through the fog. Pack frames creaking, we left camp under instrument conditions. For half an hour, we worked our way downriver until we hit the first side creek. Using its course for reference, we struggled through a mile of brush until we struck the tree line, at which point we turned up the steep sidehill to the east. After an hour of climbing, we still couldn't see anything but an amorphous ocean of gray.

When our legs told us we had reached the ridgetop, we consulted our topo map and set off on a compass bearing to the north. Navigating by compass and contour line, we made our way across the ridge for another hour until the ground began to fall away beneath us in all directions. At this point, I knew that we were either directly above Dick's bull or hopelessly lost.

As we sat down for a bite of lunch and tried to avoid thinking about the implications of the second possibility, patches of blue began to appear overhead. Terrain features emerged from the murky sea around us, and then, as suddenly as if lights had been turned on in a darkened room, the fog layer lifted away. Sunlight sparkled from the crystalline dew, highlighting a mosaic of color on the wild tundra around us. Miraculously, we were right where we were supposed to be.

Dick pointed out the creek bottom where his caribou lay in a dense cluster of willow. I set up my spotting scope and studied the area carefully for evidence of bears. While I tried to pick the brush apart around Dick's animal with my eyes, Ray was busy with his own binoculars. He quickly spotted a bachelor group of five mature bulls grazing at the head of the drainage. With no sign of troublesome visitors near Dick's kill, I swung the spotting scope down the valley and soon located another trophy-class animal grazing alone on the opposite sidehill.

It was time for a brief strategy session. Dick volunteered to take the three empty pack frames down to his animal and begin the process of boning it out. We agreed to meet there later in the afternoon to start the long pack back to camp together. In the meantime, Ray elected to head up the valley and see what he could do with the five caribou feeding there. I turned my attention in the opposite direction, studying the solitary bull's movement patterns and committing to memory as many landmarks as possible.

Alaska is a land of striking seasonal changes. Around the equinox, you can gain or lose fifteen minutes of sunlight per day. Streams that seem barren one week will be alive with salmon the next. Soon they will reek of rotten fish, only to become barren once again until the cycle of life and death begins all over. Every big game species in the north changes profoundly with the calendar, and the barren ground caribou is no exception.

If you see your first caribou during late summer, you will probably be struck, as I was years ago, by the anomaly of its coloration. At this time of year, the caribou's sleek coat is a flat metallic gray, the color of a well-worn shotgun barrel. While August caribou lack the white capes they will develop later in the season, the contrast between the mature bull's pale, flowing throat latch and dark neck is never more dramatic. That stark patch of white is often apparent from a great distance, even before one can distinguish the presence of antlers above it.

Large herds are unusual at this time of year. While the caribou migration is a sight to behold, as a bowhunter I don't particularly miss it. In fact, from the archer's perspective, it is the solitary nature of the mature bull's disposition during the pre-rut that makes late summer such an ideal time to stalk it. Large herds, with many eyes and noses, can make the final approach to bow range difficult if not impossible.

The principal factor governing caribou behavior in late summer seems to be their desire to avoid heat and bugs. In southwestern Alaska's rolling hills, they often appear skylined at the tops of the very highest ridges. While sheep hunting in the Alaska range one summer, I observed a band of caribou grazing happily among steep cliffs a thousand feet above the ram I was watching through my glasses. Flying along the foothills at this time of year, I have often seen caribou concentrated on the last remaining patches of the previous winter's snow, where they like to loll about like kids at a swimming pool.

There are some disadvantages to hunting caribou in August. You can expect to do some climbing and cover a lot of ground in search of a trophy. Heat and summer rain often make meat care difficult. Antlers are still in velvet until late August or early September, which somehow detracts from their impact when the animal is on the hoof and which obligates the successful hunter to hours of work in o rder to prepare them for even the simplest home-fashioned mount. Nonetheless, whenever I find myself perched on an outlook studying a trophy-class bull and plotting a seemingly impossible stalk to the intimate range bowhunting demands, it often occurs to me that there is no place else on earth I would rather be.

"It's bear country," I reminded Dick as we parted company on the ridge. Even though Dick lives on the edge of the Yellowstone ecosystem, grizzlies just aren't a daily fact of life anywhere in the lower forty-eight states the way they are in Alaska. "They've had a whole day to locate your dead bull," I said. "Be careful down there."

Dick checked the chamber on the .375 before starting his climb down the hill. Then he pointed to the longbow, which was all the ordnance I carried. "I think you are the one who needs to be careful," he said.

In fact, it was Ray's turn to have his bear number come up that afternoon. When he started across the tundra to investigate a "dead" grizzly, a cub jumped out of the grass and onto the chest of the carcass, which turned out to be a sow who was very much alive. Nothing much came of the encounter other than a few gray hairs for Ray, which was fortunate, since he was no better armed than I was, and the nearest climbing tree was miles away in the river bottom.

I watched Dick disappear over the edge of the hill and then set off on my own. Stalks in this sort of terrain always seem to take longer than planned. Distances are invariably deceptive in open, mountainous country, and tundra is more difficult to walk across than it looks, especially when it is interspersed with alders. I estimated that it would take me forty minutes to cross the valley to the swale where I had seen the bull earlier. An hour and a half later, I was still climbing through the last of the brush.

When I emerged from the cover at last, the bull was nowhere to be seen. If I have learned anything about bowhunting over the years, it is that blundering about aimlessly is seldom an effective tactic. With a welcome sigh of breeze in my face, I eased my way onto a shale outcropping and started to glass. It took another ten minutes of careful searching before I located my quarry. He had bedded down halfway up the hillside. Ten yards upwind from a broken strip of alders, he couldn't have picked a better resting place for my purposes if I had asked him to. Now it was time to take one last look and be certain that this was the bull I wanted.

Spotting scope and tripod braced against the wind, I zoomed in on the velvet antlers and carefully reviewed what I saw: one good shovel, symmetrical bez, decent rear points, average main beams. Good top tines more than made up for an overall lack of mass. Seven days into the hunt, this one was a keeper.

One can argue, of course, that the trophy judging of animals is a meaningless exercise. While I don't worry about record books as such, I do find formal measurement to be a useful way to quantify the fascination with horns and antlers that I share with so many other serious big game hunters. In that context, field judging heads becomes a skill to develop and enjoy just like stalking, tracking, and shooting. You certainly don't have to care about the details in order to enjoy a caribou hunt, but if you do, there are some things you should know before you set out.

The two most difficult animals to evaluate on the hoof in Alaska, if not the entire continent, are the caribou and the mountain goat. The problems these two species pose arise for totally opposite reasons. For the goat hunter, a bit of horn the size of a fingertip is the difference between a nice billy and an exceptional one. Caribou, on the other hand, sport such a riot of antler that not even the official scoring system can keep track of it.

Two other factors complicate matters further. Caribou have the highest ratio of antler to body size of any North American game animal. They *all* look big, especially to the novice. And unlike such familiar species as deer and elk, the relationship between the whole and the sum of the parts is not always readily apparent or even logical. If a whitetail looks big at first glance, he almost certainly is, although details may add or subtract somewhat from his overall measurement total. Not so with caribou. Some bulls with tremendous main beams have poorly developed shovels and bez. Specimens well represented in these departments may lack rear points, good top tines, or mass. Evaluating a head requires both good judgment and good optics. Here are a few pointers.

Don't worry much about the storied double shovel, which in fact is something of a biological anomaly. Just be sure your bull has one good one. The bez, the structure arising from the main beam just above the lower shovel, should be long and symmetrical. Rear points are a nice bonus. Top tines can add tremendously to a head's total. Remember that only the longest two count, and that asymmetry on top is both common and costly. Mass is rewarded highly and can make up for lots of deficiencies elsewhere.

And when all is said and done, remember that an animal's trophy value is ultimately in the eye of the beholder, and that any mature big game animal taken with the bow according to the standards of fair chase makes the grade. That may be the most important lesson of all.

Landmarks committed to memory down to the last detail of the alder strip through which I would make my final approach, I stashed my day pack and ran through a final equipment checklist. Broadheads: honed and razor sharp. Noisy rain gear: removed, replaced by my quietest woolens. Shooting glove and arm guard: secure. It was time to move.

I crawled back down the rocks and set off around the sidehill, navigating by a series of predetermined reference points. I didn't want to see the bull again until he was within bow range. The wind, for once, held steady in my face. As I closed within a hundred yards, it began to occur to me that I might actually pull this off.

I once made the statement in print that caribou are stupid. That was an unfortunate choice of words. I do not believe in insulting the animals that I hunt, especially those that have afforded me as much enjoyment as the caribou. *Rangifer tarandus,* I hereby apologize. Officially.

What I should have said, to put it more tactfully, is that caribou are poor problem solvers. They have evolved over the centuries to be tough rather than logical, in keeping with the nature of the demanding environment they inhabit.

Here is my own book on the barren ground caribou, derived from many hours spent at close range with them. Vision: good. Hearing: fair. Nose: superb. Overall wariness: couldn't care less, as long as you are downwind and out of "wolf range," which unfortunately is about twice as far as I can shoot a long bow with acceptable accuracy. All of which explains why the steady breeze blowing across the hill from the bedded bull to the final perimeter of brush filled me with the flush of excitement that I always feel when I realize that I might actually take a fine animal with a stick and string after a long open country stalk.

Now, finally, I am twenty-five yards away from the caribou, certain of my position because I can see velvet antler tines protruding above the last strip of brush that separates us. Although the bull is technically within bow range, our proximity isn't doing me much good. He is still bedded, offering an impossible target of muscle and bone, and there are too many obstructions between us for a clear shot. It is time to start bowhunting seriously.

I can see where I want to be, fifteen yards away through the alders. By the orientation of his antlers, it is apparent that the bull is facing away from me down the valley. By now, the wind in my face seems as reliable as an old friend. I have a watch, and it occurs to me that it might be interesting to see how long it takes to cover fifteen yards. I decide not to look, however. Events like this are best left to their own timetables. After plotting my route twig by twig, I nock an arrow, ease my bow ahead of me, and start to crawl.

With no sensation of time's passage, I arrive at my destination three bow lengths from the bull. Now there is no more brush between us, but he is still bedded down, leaving me no target but neck and shoulder. There is nothing to do but wait. Since they depend on low-quality table fare for their survival, caribou are very active ruminants, and I can plainly hear the bull belching and growling from my hiding place. Clouds have blown back in. A light rain starts to fall. A raptor sails by overhead, *kreeing* at some unseen companion. I try not to think about the sun arcing its way through the clouds toward the distant western horizon, and the long hike back to the camp. I also remind myself that point-blank shots with the bow demand the same mental discipline as all the others do.

Then suddenly he is up on all fours, a huge gray mass of hide and antler. I make myself ignore the headgear and focus on a spot just in back of the shoulder. He swings his head toward me but doesn't see. Then he turns again and stares back down the valley in search of something known only to caribou. To this day I have no recollection of drawing the bow or releasing the arrow.

The only indication of contact is a soft *thwit,* the sound a bandage makes when it is pulled suddenly from the skin. The bull runs off down the hill with the peculiar splay-legged trot that resembles the gait of no other animal that I know. Forty yards. Sixty yards. Come on. Eighty yards away, he hesitates, hindquarters suddenly uncertain, then folds himself into the tundra for the last time.

I slump backwards into a cushion of lichens and moss, breathing easily at last, and listen to the sound of the wind overhead, and to the beating of my heart.

Zen in the Art of Bear Hunting

FROM THE BOWHUNTER'S perspective, there are two kinds of seaweed to be found along the beaches of southeast Alaska: popcorn and salad.

Popcorn is the more interesting of the two in spite of the problems that it causes. The key structural feature is the tiny air bladder that keeps its fronds aloft as the tide washes in and out. At low water, popcorn lies innocently along the beaches where the bears prowl each spring, so quiet and innocuous that you will scarcely notice the stuff until you step on it, at which point the force of a boot against all those little air sacs will make a quiet beach explode like a Chinese New Year parade. The ensuing snap, crackle, and pop will be audible for hundreds of yards and is guaranteed to send whatever you were stalking into the security of the everpresent rain forest jungle.

Salad is friendlier stuff. Heaped up in thick, gelatinous piles of glop, normal conditions of rainfall and tide keep it moist enough to consume the sound of even a carelessly placed step. When stalking bears along a crunchy beach, the observant bowhunter soon learns to keep his boots in the salad whenever possible.

At five o'clock in the afternoon on one recent Alaska bear hunt, I was in the salad. Unfortunately, I wasn't standing in it. I was lying on my belly, virtually buried in wet seaweed like a lobster on the way to market. Since I had been prone and still for some time, my woolens had soaked through, and it was all I could do to ignore the hostile marine life crawling toward my skin.

Ahead of me on the beach, a patch of new grass the size of my living room floor stood between the high water line and the edge of the jungle. This was bear grass—not the true bear grass of the mountain west, but the stuff my hunting partners and I call bear grass for reasons that will soon become clear. In the middle of this green splash, a black bear grazed delicately. Although not huge by coastal Alaska standards, he was a mature boar in the three hundred-pound class. With a prime unrubbed hide, he was certainly big enough for me during the waning hours of a long hunt.

A shore bird skittered down the log that I lay behind, passing inches from my nose. Salad squished beneath me as I shifted my weight furtively. Suddenly I found myself wondering why a responsible family man with no history of mental illness would choose to spend a wind-driven afternoon buried in wet seaweed watching a black bear eat grass.

Why indeed?

Thousands of years ago, a collision of tectonic plates blasted Alaska's coastal mountain range up from the floor of the Pacific rim. Things haven't settled down much since then. This coastline is still a land of violent, beautiful extremes. Attempt to describe it and you will immediately find yourself knee-deep in superlatives. Climate? The wettest, nastiest, most unpredictable. Terrain? The steepest, brushiest, least forgiving. Tides? The highest, lowest, strongest in between.

And it is the climate, the terrain, and the tides that define the bowhunting experience in coastal Alaska. The weather can be challenging or depressing, depending on how long you have been out in it and how wet it has left you. Even at its occasional sunny best, fluctuating wind currents pose a constant threat to the most carefully planned stalks. Between the beach and the alpine, the forest is often so dense that walking is difficult, and hunting impossible. The tides take some getting used to. Changing fifteen feet or so every six hours, they make beaches and flats appear and disappear as if by magic. It is these tide flats that yield a new growth of forbs and grasses each spring, which in turn draw the bears from the security of the impenetrable jungle to feed.

The bear grass is just the first course in the ursine seasonal cuisine. For true omnivores like bears (and bear hunters) coastal Alaska is just one vast smorgasbord. After the bruins have primed their digestive tracts with vegetation, it is only a matter of time until salmon return to fresh water. Throughout the summer, almost every stream along the coast is stuffed with goodies from the sea at one time or another. Then as the runs of pinks, reds and silvers start to taper off, the berries begin to ripen. Considering this rich diet, it is little wonder that these are the largest black bears in the world.

On the first day of this particular hunt, Ray Stalmaster and Doug Borland set off in a skiff to explore a new steelhead stream. After studying our maps and charts, Tom Budde and I loaded the second skiff and headed toward a rocky bay that offered the possibility of both fish and bears. Fly rods in hand, we spent several hours thrashing our way up the stream at the head of the bay without turning a fish. By late afternoon, we were ready for some leisure activity like bowhunting dangerous game.

After Tom and I parted company at the skiff, I slogged across the creek on an outgoing tide and positioned myself at the downwind corner of a large grass flat. A second stream emerged from the woods a half-mile away, and the tidal basin between my position and the stream mouth looked like ideal spring bear habitat. We were early this year, and the new growth was just beginning to appear in the brown decay of last year's grass crop. I noted, however, that the tips of the new grass blades were chewed off squarely, a certain sign that bears were indeed using the area.

Alaska had experienced an unusually dry spring that year. The sun was shining as it had been all week, and I soon found myself settled against a mossy log enjoying the warmth of the afternoon. I spent several minutes trying to pick devil's club thorns from my hands and then turned my attention to the tide flat. The basin in front of me was full of migrating water birds, and I picked up my binoculars to enjoy the spectacle. My field of vision swept across cormorants, mergansers, and otters, and then suddenly there he was, a fluid five hundred-pound lump of coal on the vivid green background of the flat. My lazy afternoon was over.

No matter how many times I experience the sight, whenever I see a bear in the wild my perception of the natural world and my own place in it changes just a little. It doesn't matter whether the bear is large or small, black or grizzly. I have spent my share of time at close range to bears and all but a minute or so of that time has been peaceful, but the simple presence of a bear is enough to undo the illusion that man is in complete command of his environment. Each and every one serves as a reminder that there are mysterious forces afoot in the world—Melville's whale or Faulkner's bear. When bears stop giving me that tingling feeling, I'm going to stop hunting and check into a nursing home.

As I watched, the huge bear walked across the head of the grass flat, an area I had yet to explore. At first I thought he might just disappear into the jungle, but then he stopped at the edge of the flat to feed. With a favorable wind in my face, I set off to close the distance between us.

The low tide allowed me to walk directly across the salt water basin. The bear continued to browse in an open copse of evergreens. The second fresh water stream emerged from the forest and meandered across the flat. I used the stream's even gravel bottom and background noise to close easily to a range of sixty yards from the bear. Then I made my first tactical error. A series of shallow tide guts meandered between the creek and the tree line. Their mud banks offered quiet footing and what seemed to be a sure route to a shooting position. Without hesitation, I started up the nearest gut.

Twenty yards later, I was out of cover—and out of bow range. With the wind in my face and the bear's attention focused underfoot upon his dinner, the distance that I needed seemed so tantalizingly close. Without reviewing my options, I nocked an arrow and started to move.

I had overlooked the effects of the dry spring upon the grass, which was as dry as excelsior beneath my suddenly awkward boots. Even the gentlest footstep produced a slow, agonizing crunch. Who would ever imagine that an Alaska bowhunter could miss the rain?

Five paces ahead, the remains of an empty tide pool promised relief from the noisy footing and an easy crawl to shooting range. As carefully as possible, I crept forward. After all, I only needed five more steps.

I didn't get them. Intent upon the bear, I was halfway home when I stepped on a dry branch concealed by the grass. The sound of twigs breaking rose above the quiet of the afternoon like a bad joke. The bear made two quick bounds and disappeared into the jungle.

I rose slowly from my awkward, half-crouched position. The flat seemed barren and still, but only because I had been concentrating so intently on the bear. Now the sounds of the birds and the breeze in the timber seemed to return in measures, although they had really been there all along. I realized how the mental demands of the stalk had narrowed my own perceptions, and how that narrowing had been an illusion.

I walked slowly into the glade where the bear had stood and tried to determine what I might have done differently. The answer was apparent at once, as soon as I stopped to look and think. The little creek curved sharply as it entered the trees. At its nearest point, its bank was only a few yards from the bear's position. Had I taken the time to analyze my position, the creek bed would have allowed me easy access to point-blank range.

There was a lesson to be learned from all this, as there is at the end of any stalk. I had been a victim of my own arrogance. I had closed my mind to the flat's possibilities and I had underestimated the acuity of the bear. You can't bowhunt arrogantly, I told myself as I turned to race the tide back to the skiff. It seemed simple enough.

The seven days between the first stalk and the last were hardly un-eventful. We explored new country and caught steelhead until we ran out of flies. The weather turned from severe clear to typical southeast Alaska grunge. No one shot a bear.

Spray was flying over the bow of the skiff as Ray and I pulled away from our favorite steelhead stream for our final afternoon of bear hunting. We cruised an outside beach for an hour looking for game, but accomplished nothing except to get ourselves and everything we owned soaking wet. We finally gave up and pulled into the lee of a rocky point to warm up and glass a stretch of beach a large boar had been working all week.

You can learn a lot about a civilization by walking along its mean high water line. As I circled the point gathering firewood, I was reminded again, as I had been all week, that our own produces a staggering amount of junk. While it seemed totally alien to this wild and beautiful place, plastic artifacts lay everywhere: bottles, boxes, wrappers, rope, pieces of netting. The lettering on the jetsam spoke in a dozen different languages. This was the legacy of decades of environmental disregard on the part of my own species, and it was hardly a source of pride.

Temporarily saddened by all this, I was leaning over a pile of damp kindling trying to coax a fire to life when Ray saw the bear. As we studied him through the glasses to confirm his trophy quality and the absence of cubs, Ray graciously offered me the stalk. Moments later, I set off down the beach.

This was different terrain than the sheltered flat where I had made the first stalk of the hunt. Exposed constantly to the elements, the ocean beach was nothing but a narrow strip of weathered rock wedged between the high water line and the jungle. Huge drift logs, escapees from years' worth of broken log booms, lay everywhere like jackstraws. Little patches of grass managed to sprout forth here and there, and that was enough to interest the bear.

I closed the first three hundred yards quickly. The bear was basically feeding away from me, clambering easily over the tangle of logs with only an occasional pause to root out some tide line delicacy. As I began to overtake him, I became aware of the gravel's crunch beneath my boots and noticed also that the beach here was covered with the ever treacherous popcorn.

I paused and wriggled out of my waders. The drift logs offered a route over the noisy hazards of the beach, and I found that in my stocking feet I could sprint along them almost soundlessly. Whenever the bear turned away from me and moved, I moved too, scampering like an otter along the logs. The bear and I covered half a mile of beachfront property together like this, but I just couldn't get within bow range.

Finally, to the relief of my unprotected feet, the bear found what he wanted: a lush patch of genuine Alaska bear grass. For the first time all afternoon, I wasn't trying to play catch up. A large boulder lay on the beach halfway between the last drift log and the feeding bear. With the wind still blowing straight down the beach, I had no trouble reaching the rock. The bear was forty yards away.

I eased a shaft onto my bow string and waited. The patch of grass ran within good bow range of my hiding place. The bear was grazing about in random circles, and if he moved along the closest edge of the grass patch, I would have an ideal shot.

If, of course, is one of bowhunting's golden words. After fifteen minutes of aimless feeding, the bear flopped down in the middle of the grass. Facing me head on, he was ten yards beyond my range and offered nothing but head and shoulder, an impossible target for an archer.

It has been my experience that the best solution to such Mexican standoffs in the field is patience, but failing light and incoming tide told me that the meter was running. Ten feet from the security of the boulder, a long, narrow log lay embedded in the gravel. It ran obliquely toward the bear and offered a possible route to the range that I needed. When the bear reached back over his shoulder to rake in another mouthful of dinner, I scrambled for the log and started to crawl.

And that is how I wound up in the salad.

Black bear cubs are genuinely cute animals. Tumbling around the woods after their mothers, they always look like something you could take home and give to one of your kids for a birthday present. Yearlings retain a certain amount of that cuteness, and even young adults look like jokers at heart most of the time. Somewhere around the three hundred-pound mark, however, black bears stop looking cuddly. Because Alaska outdoorsmen spend so much of their time fretting about grizzlies, they tend to become casual about their smaller black cousins. This is a mistake. A seven-foot black bear is a very impressive animal, especially when appreciated at close range.

Because of the log's angle, it took me twenty yards of crawling to get five yards closer to the bear. I could hear him chewing by now, a rhythmic, bovine noise that seemed wholly out of place on the beach. Buried unevenly in the sand, the log was giving me progressively less cover as I advanced. Even though I kept my profile as low as possible while I crawled, I knew that my back was starting to show over the top of the log. Suddenly, the bear stopped chewing.

One of the true pleasures of stalking bears with the bow comes from the flavor of excitement that hunting dangerous game provides. You can tell yourself that they are just big Black Angus cattle, for that is the mental fiction you need to maintain in order to get yourself within bow range, but there is always another more primitive part of the brain that recognizes this construction as nonsense. This flight or fight tingle is something quite different than the excitement you feel when you come to draw twenty yards from a deer or a moose, and it is something you will never truly experience if you do your bear hunting fifteen feet up in the air from a tree stand.

I rose slowly and peered over the top of the log. The bear had risen to his feet. He began to pace back and forth angrily, never taking his eyes away from my position. He was at the outer limits of my range, and I doubted he would stand still and offer me his broadside if I rose further and came to draw. With the wind still in my favor, the bear had no idea what I was. I began to wonder what would happen if he decided to wander over and take a look. This was the sort of situation that back-up firearms are meant to address. Unfortunately, my pistol was right where it always is at this stage of a stalk: a mile down the beach in the bottom of my day pack.

In wilderness settings, bears seldom seem to spook badly from visual cues alone. Since he could not smell me, my quarry appeared more curious than concerned. After several minutes of scrutiny, he lowered his head and began to feed once more. I made a mental commitment: if he turned and opened up his side to me, I would rise to one knee and take the shot.

There was the *if* word again. If the wind blew steadily along the beaches of Alaska, my living room wall would be three-deep in bear rugs. Weather patterns and rugged terrain guarantee that it almost never does. I had been unusually lucky on this stalk already in this regard, and I knew it. The first sign of trouble was the vague sensation that something was missing. It took me a moment to realize that the something was the feel of the breeze in my face. Suddenly, the bear's massive head shot up from the grass and his eyes squinted shut as he sampled the air. Helplessly, as if watching an accident in progress, I felt the wind swing onshore and quarter behind me. Then the grass flat was empty. The sound of brush breaking rose from the jungle as the bear tore into the cover, and then there was nothing left but the sound of the ocean and the treacherous wind.

I rose from the salad and let my nerves spool down for a minute before I began to critique the stalk. I paced off the distances from the boulder and the log to the bear's various positions. My estimates had been correct: I really had needed another five or ten yards for a certain shot. No regrets there. I realized that I should have been more aggressive. The wind and the bear's behavior both spoke of the need for positive action. I had let the bear intimidate me into being passive. I needed to be more . . . arrogant. After all, you can't bowhunt bears without a proper measure of arrogance.

Now, wait a minute . . .

And that is how this hunt ends, not with the traditional bearskin rug, but with a puzzle, a Zen *koan* if you will.

I have a long-standing complaint against outdoor writers in general and many bowhunting writers in particular. I object to the implication that all good hunts must end with a trophy on the wall, and I object to the assumption put forth by some that the tally of animals collected can somehow be used to quantify the worth of the hunt (not to mention the hunter). These things cannot possibly be true.

Don't misunderstand me. I like reading good stories about good animals taken fairly with the bow. I like it even better when I get to write one. But it is a fact that bowhunting involves many more attempts than realizations. Even the most highly skilled practitioners of this most difficult art come out of the woods empty handed far more often than not.

So what? Well, as long-time hunting partner Ray Stalmaster once observed one winter day halfway up a tall mountain: "If you are going to enjoy cross-country skiing, you better learn to enjoy going up hill." By the same token, if you are going to enjoy bowhunting, you had best learn to enjoy belly crawling even if you come up short, because most of the time, you will.

In fact, every stalk has something to offer, no matter what its outcome. It wasn't until I began to feel comfortable with this notion that I really felt like a bowhunter. There comes a point when each of us has to decide whether we are more interested in shooting bears or hunting them, and from that decision a whole series of choices about hunting equipment and methods eventually follows. Technical solutions to the problem of a bear forty yards away certainly exist, even for the bowhunter. Taking such an approach might well have gotten my bear tag out of my pocket and onto my quarry's hide, but look what I would have missed.

Of course, hunts like this never really end. The bears are still out there, and if we can keep our tanker captains sober and our appetite for cheap wood products under control, they probably always will be. As surely as the tides rise and fall, the bears will stir in their dens next spring, emerge blinking into the sunlight, and head for the tide flats again.

I already have the dates circled on my calendar.

THREE ————————————————————————

Kid Stuff

HERE ABOVE THE timberline, the mountains of southeastern Alaska are covered in nearly unnatural shades of green. These are not the greens of a birch forest in springtime or a stand of pines in the early morning light. Not even close. The greens of the coastal Alaska alpine are neon greens; intense, reflective, the purest essence of the chlorophyl that traps the sun's energy and begins the food chain that feeds us all.

I suspect that the weather has something to do with it. That is the rain forest down there below us, after all. Perhaps the plant life here just sees so little of the sun that when it does appear, it must be ready to absorb every photon of solar energy that comes down the line. When the sun shines here, this country looks like it means business.

Tales of southeast Alaska's rain are legendary. Parts of this area receive two hundred inches of the cold gray stuff every year—and that is a lot of rain by anyone's standards. Local residents get philosophical about wet weather. Visitors mostly just get wet. What everyone gets, wherever their home of record, is a childish excitement on these rare sunny days. Even hardened loggers and barnacle-encrusted commercial fishermen start acting like kids on summer vacation when the rain breaks, the clouds roll back, and the sun beams down to reveal the sea and the mountains that make this area such a special part of the natural world.

And so it had been for nearly a week. I had warned Ray and his son Joe all about the weather before they left Montana. I had explained that we would be living in our rubber boots, that down would be useless, that layers of rain flies were necessary for any sort of outdoor camping. The sun had made a liar out of me so far, but I wasn't complaining. The weather scarcely mattered to Joe anyway, since he and my own son, Nick,

18

had gotten every item of clothing they owned soaking wet within twenty-four hours of our arrival. Those who have kids of their own, or who can remember being kids themselves, will require no explanation.

We had spent the first part of the week fishing near sea level. It was August, and the rivers were full of pink salmon, with enough fifteen-pound silvers thrown in to keep matters interesting. Attacking the clear waters of some favorite streams with their fly rods quite literally from dawn to dark, the boys seemed incapable of fatigue. It was rejuvenating just to watch them, as anyone who can remember spending a summer at ease with a fishing rod and no other agenda will again understand. In between salmon streams, we had launched our inflatable boat in the salt water often enough to fill our ice chest with halibut and cod fillets. Now, finally, it was time to go hunting.

The previous evening, we had flown in to a lake at the fifteen hundred-foot level and set up camp in an old Forest Service cabin. The roof looked like an original Civilian Conservation Corps project, and it did not inspire my confidence in the event of serious southeast Alaska weather. However, there had been nothing but stars overhead the previous evening as we finished a meal of beer-batter halibut, and we had just awakened to a crisp dew fall and the play of the early morning sunlight upon that incredible expanse of green in the mountains above us. If I were to ask Alaska to serve us up a custom order morning to begin a wilderness hunt, I couldn't imagine getting a better one.

Our quarry was the reclusive and underappreciated Sitka blacktailed deer. Derived distantly from whitetail ancestors, as are all New World deer, the Sitka blacktail is a primitive subspecies that nature essentially left alone in the isolated wilderness of what is now southeast Alaska while evolutionary forces elsewhere created the Colombian blacktail, the modern version of the whitetail and its various subspecies, and the great hybrid of the deer family, the mule deer. The Sitka blacktail missed out on all this adaptive diversity and simply went about its business over the centuries, all but cut off from its cousins by its isolated habitat. There is no easy way into or out of southeast Alaska for man or animal alike.

And so, while it may be convenient to think of the Sitka blacktail as just an undersized mule deer, that concept hardly does justice to its unique biological credentials. In fact, because it has evolved less from primitive whitetail ancestors than have other blacktail races, in some ways it resembles the whitetail more. Its tail looks like a whitetail's that has been airbrushed lightly with black ink around the edges. It has the smallest metatarsal glands of any blacktail subspecies, and it runs without the mule deer's characteristic stotting gate. And while its branching antler structure resembles a mule deer's, its facial mask is distinctive. Anyone who regards the Sitka blacktail as just another deer is missing the point of hunting them.

Despite these unique characteristics, Alaska's only deer species generally doesn't get the respect it deserves as a big game animal. Much of the problem stems from its competition. Most bowhunters who travel north have more exotic game than deer on their agenda. When I moved to Alaska, I was so infatuated with moose, bears, caribou, and sheep that I couldn't even think about deer hunting for several years, and when I finally did, I usually just went back to Montana to hunt whitetails with my old friends. Of course, that was an oversight on my part, as I finally discovered. Paradoxically, Alaska's deer are more narrowly distributed than most of the state's other big game species, since they inhabit a limited coastal range in the southeastern panhandle, Prince William Sound, and the Kodiak Island area. It takes just as much effort to go deer hunting in Alaska as it does to go sheep hunting, which, if you stop to think about it, should serve to make the Sitka blacktail even more special as a quarry.

Since we weren't familiar with the terrain, we made a leisurely start that first morning so that we could see where we were going in good daylight. That's always a sound policy when hunting in mountainous areas, no matter how eager you are to get going. In the long run, a careful orientation to new country saves wasted effort that can be better used pursuing game. We took our time, checked some topo maps, and packed a lunch. Finally, Ray and Joe set off up the mountain in back of camp while Nick and I started to work our way around the lake in the opposite direction.

Although there was a lot of hilly terrain to deal with, it was basically pleasant hiking as long as we stayed in the alpine and avoided the alders. Nick was one year short of legal hunting age that season, but he made an excellent companion. He was full of questions, and I was glad to see that he was interested in learning to do things right. After an hour and a half of climbing, we emerged onto a boulder-strewn ridgeline and started to glass. We immediately spotted a large male black bear feeding on berries several hundred yards below us. Unfortunately, bear season didn't open for a week. There was no prohibition against watching, however, and we did just that for over an hour.

We finally located the first deer of the trip, a cluster of does and fawns feeding in an avalanche chute a mile away up the mountain. It would have been a challenging hike to their position, and I was almost thankful that I didn't see the antlers that would have made me try it. Instead, we contented ourselves with watching the bear and picking enough blueberries to guarantee a major pancake feed the following morning.

By early afternoon, I could see streamers of fog welling over the lips of the ridges to the west, where the cold Pacific lay. I had spent enough time in this country to know exactly what that meant. Just as I finished giving Nick a quick course in compass bearings and topo map orientation, the lights went out. We picked our way slowly back down the ridge through the soup. It wasn't a particularly difficult bit of navigation, but the visibility was poor enough to get the little voice in the back of my brain asking *what if?* I'll admit that I never really told Nick how glad I was to see the cabin emerge from the gloom in front of us.

Ray and Joe arrived in camp an hour later. As I fired up the stove and started to fry the last of the fish fillets, they briefed us on the details of their day. They had found a steep but reasonable trail up the mountain behind the cabin, which led to a huge open expanse of alpine. They, too, had seen bears, and Joe had even managed to stalk a small buck in the fog. We agreed that we would start before dawn the next day and hike up the mountain together for a day of serious hunting.

That is just where shooting light found us the following morning, high above the lake and the cabin, watching the sunlight fill a long series of alpine basins with those marvelous shades of green. Ray and Joe wanted to hunt their way around the ridgeline and return to the cabin by an untested route. Nick and I decided to spend the day hunting the back side of the mountain, where broken terrain and dozens of alpine meadows offered good conditions for glassing and stalking. We agreed to meet at the cabin at the end of the day, and I watched them set off uphill.

Joe looked ready to take his first buck. He has always been a precocious hunter, demonstrating patience and woods savvy beyond his years. He is an absolute natural with the longbow as well, and had terrified the gophers and rock chucks around his country home for years. Ray himself is a hard hunter, but I knew that as much as he wanted to take a representative blacktail on this trip, he wanted to see his son take one even more. The two of them looked as if they were meant to hunt together as they started up the ridge. I couldn't help remembering my own childhood and the way my father patiently introduced me to the joys of wild places.

Nick and I spent the day hiking and glassing. As you and your children age together, there comes a time when they are getting bigger and stronger while you are merely getting older. I realized that day that the lines representing our physical capacities were about to cross. Nick kept scampering ahead across the rocks like an eager young puppy while I brought up the rear. I told myself that I was going slowly so that I could hunt more carefully, but that was only true in part. Wait until he gets a pack full of venison on his shoulders, I told myself. I hoped that we would get a chance to test my theory, if only to prove it incorrect.

We saw no fewer than six trophy–class black bears that day, all with their heads down in the berries looking ever so stalkable. I had some silent words with myself for planning the trip a week too early to catch the bear season, but there was nothing to do except enjoy watching them. We saw deer that day as well, but not the buck I wanted. Although we had nothing with us but blueberries and sore muscles when we arrived back in camp that night, it was hard to imagine that the day had been anything less than a success.

I had some reservations about the descent Ray had planned on his circular route back to camp, so I was relieved to see him emerge from the brush half an hour later and start up the last little hill to the cabin with Joe trailing close behind him. As they drew nearer, I made several interesting observations. Ray was carrying a broken longbow. Joe had a velvet blacktail rack lashed to the top of his day pack. Most important of all, they were both smiling. Since the last of the halibut was gone, there was no use saving any beer-batter ingredients and I sent Nick down to the lake for a couple of cold ones. I knew there were tales to tell that night. After Ray and Joe struggled out of their boots and packs, we sat down in front of the cabin with the light fading from the peaks around us and listened to Ray tell them.

They had made good progress through the alpine tundra after leaving us that morning. They were sitting on a rock high atop the ridge glassing and eating lunch when Ray looked down in horror to see his favorite longbow delaminate right in front of him. The ultimate cause of this tragedy is still unclear. I suspect that the demands of too many Alaska hunts in difficult climatic conditions had simply taken their inevitable toll, although it is certainly hard to imagine a less convenient time of reckoning. At any rate, there sat Ray, high on top of a mountain in the middle of prime hunting country, reduced to the status of observer.

Ray has always had a good attitude toward setbacks, and as it turned out there was plenty to observe that day. The deer must have been taking advantage of the good weather, for Ray and Joe soon spotted a group of a dozen feeding below them, including one three-point buck. They discussed strategy briefly, and then Joe began his stalk.

Rolling terrain and a friendly wind allowed a fairly easy approach to sixty yards, but then the going got tough. Alpine tundra is ankle-deep at best, and the presence of a dozen different sets of eyes didn't help matters either. Nonetheless, Joe moved forward methodically, literally one inch at a time. He has had great respect for the limitations of our equipment drilled into him, and he wasn't about to take a shot over twenty-five yards, no matter how great the temptation. It took him an hour to close from sixty yards to forty yards from the buck. At this point, one of the does finally caught him moving a foot midstride, and the deer scampered away down the mountain.

Ray freely admits that he would have given up at this point, but Joe kept right on hunting. These were wilderness deer who had never seen human predators before, and a hundred yards down the mountain they all stopped and began to graze once more. Joe was able to move in among them once again, relying on no tricks other than patience and youthful optimism. Twice more he spooked the deer temporarily, only to have them settle down again and allow him another approach. It is Ray's theory that after three hours of this, they finally decided to accept Joe as some harmless natural phenomenon. On his fourth approach, he closed to the twenty-yard range from the buck that he had been trying for all along. From there, he sent one of his little cedar arrows into the three-point's neck for a perfect one-shot kill.

One characteristic of the Sitka blacktail that most Alaska outdoorsmen are familiar with is its quality on the table. Up north, moose is a staple, caribou delicious, and sheep meat legendary. According to many wild game enthusiasts, however, the Sitka blacktail tops them all. I had emphasized this point to Ray and Joe earlier, and was delighted to see that they had packed the loins off the mountain with them that night in their day packs. In fact, because of the warm weather, they had buried the rest of the venison in an ice cave they had discovered on top of the ridge, leaving us a little bit of packing responsibility for the following day.

I soon had some of the best steaks known to man sizzling in a skillet over the stove. While I cooked, Ray assembled my take down recurve. I had carried this bow around for backup on more wilderness trips than I can remember, and in a way I was glad that all that effort had finally been justified. Ray wondered aloud at his ability to shoot the recurve, since both of us hunt almost exclusively with the longbow. No problem, I told him. Just pick a spot. It all sounds so easy.

The following morning, we headed back up the mountain. It was our last day of hunting, so we all carried backpacks in order to pack out the rest of Joe's buck along with anything else we might harvest. Ray was also carrying my unfamiliar recurve. Halfway up the mountain, I suddenly glimpsed something out of place in the brush to our right. Incredibly enough, a fork-horn blacktail was standing broadside barely fifteen yards away. With our hunting time down to hours, he looked heaven sent to me. I made a sharp hiss between my teeth. Ray has been through enough of these charades with me to know exactly what that meant. He froze at the head of the column and the kids took their cue from him. As slowly as possible, I eased an arrow out of my bow quiver and onto the string. By then, everyone had seen the deer. Finally the young buck took the two steps forward that brought his chest free of the brush, and I picked my spot.

Perhaps it was the backpack and perhaps it was the audience, a distraction that bowhunters seldom have to deal with. Whatever the case, I drew, anchored, and sent the arrow whistling right over the top of the deer's back. It must have traveled a mile over the cliffs before falling into the rain forest canopy far below. The deer bounded away across the hillside as I lowered my bow in stunned silence. "Dad," Nick said after a discreet interval, "I think you missed."

Well, son, right you were. And this was not an ordinary miss, either. This was a fifteen-yard miss at an animal standing broadside. With three people watching, no less, any one of whom would likely have made the same shot blindfolded. By any reasonable standards, this was a world-class miss. As you might imagine, I still hear about that shot from time to time, and probably will for years to come.

The day wasn't over yet, however. On the top of the mountain, Ray finally saw the buck we had both been looking for all along, a beautiful, heavy-beamed four by four. He made a picture-perfect stalk as the deer fed toward him. When the buck finally walked over the last contour line between them, he needed only to look left to allow Ray to draw and kill him with an eight-yard shot. Of course, he looked to his right instead, saw Ray, and immediately bounced away across the grass. Fortunately, he stopped just under thirty yards away and looked back. Unfortunately,

Ray was shooting my recurve. At least that was the excuse he used when we analyzed his miss over lunch.

The boys listened patiently as we rambled on about "Well, that's bowhunting." The fact was that they had outfished us, outhiked us, and finally outshot us, but they were too polite to point any of this out. I remembered my own father telling me years ago that he would rather see me shoot one than shoot one himself, and I finally understood what he had been talking about. I felt as if some baton had been passed up there on the mountain that week, and the process seemed as natural, inevitable, and ultimately welcome as the process of the hunt itself. I for one was glad.

Sitka blacktails? I reply when people ask me about hunting deer in Alaska. *Why, they're kid stuff.*

FOUR

A Bull from the Burn

NOWHERE IN NATURE is there a look quite as doleful as that of a suspicious cow moose. This expression doesn't have the intensity of a whitetail doe's hard stare or the penetrating contempt of a cow elk's spiteful eye, but it can make an impression nonetheless. The cow moose's look is slow and patient. The eyes seem lost in that impossibly long face as the huge nostrils test the air and inquiring ears rotate atop the great head like radar beacons. Despite its almost comical quality, this look is one that moose hunters eventually learn to treat with respect, especially when hunting with the bow.

Three days into this hunt, I was getting a full measure of the look. The cow was twenty yards away. Just beyond her, palmated antlers rocked gently back and forth as the bull I had been stalking all morning fed on, oblivious to the silent confrontation in front of him. I tried not to think about the bull and I tried not to think about the wind, which had been flirting with every point on the compass since daybreak. There was nothing left for me to do now but lie prone and motionless in the wet grass and hope that I passed muster.

The things a guy will do, I found myself thinking as moisture seeped through my clothing and the cow stared on relentlessly. *The things a guy will do to shoot a moose with a bow.*

It is not unusual to travel between Alaska and the lower forty-eight to harvest a moose. The unusual thing about this hunt was that I was making the commute in reverse. Despite having lived for several years on the very edge of Theodore Roosevelt's beloved Kenai National Moose Range, I had never killed a moose with the bow. How could an experienced bowhunter living in the world's best moose habitat fail such an elementary mission? As someone once said, let me count the ways.

26

First, there was the unfortunate matter of timing. August is the prime season to hunt my two favorite Alaska big game animals, caribou and sheep. By the time moose season rolled around in September, I was usually too busy repairing airplanes, making amends to my wife, and paying attention to my neglected medical practice to mount major expeditions into the bush. Furthermore, the presence of sixty-inch bull moose in my own back yard led to the logical conclusion that this would be a good place to hunt them. Only after several years of experience did I acknowledge that, in Alaska, hunting anything anywhere other people can drive is a waste of time.

When I finally did get serious about getting a trophy moose with the bow, there followed a series of blunders and misadventures worthy of an epic tragedy (or an epic comedy, depending on your point of view). I remember, for example, the evening I was riding alone from our high country moose camp when I rounded a bend to find a bull moose in full rut straddling the trail. As I eased out of the saddle, the bull eyed my horse and grunted belligerently a mere forty yards away. Fingers trembling, I assembled my take down recurve and eased a broadhead from the protective case behind my saddle. Across the horse's withers, I could see the bull advancing. Although not a large moose, he looked ominous enough as he paused every few steps to work the brush with his antlers. Just as I managed to get an arrow on the bowstring, my trusty quarter horse realized that whether the bull's plans involved love or war, he was the objective. I emerged from the ensuing explosion of hooves and saddle gear to find the meadow empty of large animals, wild and domestic. Since all of my own body parts were still functioning and I didn't have any broadhead holes in my hide, I decided that I had no real grounds to complain.

And then there was the time I was floating down a river in southwestern Alaska, again during the peak of the rut, when I saw a bull moose swim the current in front of me and disappear into a brushy slough. I beached my raft, readied my gear, and eased into the willows with the wind in my face. My first cow call produced an immediate belch from the cover in front of me, and within a few minutes I could hear the bull breathing in the bushes less than thirty yards away. I moaned again and a dark form appeared well within bow range, screened only by a final curtain of brush. After a long wait with no shot opportunity, I decided to bring things to a head. With a silent apology to bowyer Dick Robertson, I whacked my longbow against a branch and issued the guttural challenge of a rival bull. As my quarry tore from the cover, jumped back into the river, and swam away for all he was worth, I noticed a detail that I had overlooked at first sight. Despite the fact that the rut was well under way, this bull was still in full velvet. I will never know the exact nature of his hormonal problem, but one thing was certain: coming home to mama had been a lot more appealing than fighting with her new boyfriend!

One September afternoon during my last season in Alaska, I was certain that my jinx was about to be broken. After spotting near the timberline a large bull with a harem of cows, I worked my way into position a hundred yards downwind with ease. My first grunt brought an immediate response from the bull, who started down the mountainside in a frenzy. Then I heard the drone of an approaching aircraft. The bull was forty yards away and closing when the Super Cub driver spotted him and banked hard for a better look at his headgear. Rutting moose will tolerate all kinds of distractions, but low-level strafing runs are not among them. It was only then, as the herd stampeded down the mountain and I shook my fist at the sky, that I realized that I was about to leave the forty-ninth state without a moose notch on my bow.

There was no shortage of excuses. There were moose I didn't try for because they were too small or too far from a spot that could be reached by horse, boat, or airplane. There was the afternoon that I called three trophy-class bulls into bow range—the day after the season closed. The bottom line was that moose had become a peculiar personal nemesis.

Strange, isn't it? After all, moose are ungainly, nearsighted, lumbering giants. They are pushovers, the patsies of the North American deer clan. Right?

Wrong. Those who subscribe to the dumb-as-a-post theory of *Alces alces* have likely never seen a moose outside of a zoo, cartoon, or national park. They have certainly never hunted them in the wild with bow and arrow.

Granted, moose are not whitetails. However, there is nothing wrong with their noses, and their eyesight is quite respectable despite their sometimes myopic appearance. Their hearing is truly remarkable, since moose have adapted over time to the need to communicate with one another in the dense boreal forests that they call home. The huge distance between their ears—the greatest of any New World ungulate—allows them excellent binaural discrimination. That is the property responsible for the ability to localize sounds. Make no mistake about it: pop a twig within bow range of a moose and he will have you on his radar at once. The moose's top-heavy, bandy-legged gait may look awkward, but, as is the case with his hearing, his means of locomotion is the product of countless years of adaptation to a unique environment, as you will discover the first time you set out to track one across a swamp laced with blow downs. Consider all of these characteristics, factor in the demands of the terrain that moose inhabit, and you may finally come to agree with my opinion that the moose is one of North America's most underrated challenges with the bow.

While moose are Alaska's most popular big game animals, they enjoy a considerably more exotic reputation in the lower forty-eight states. In the mountain west, they are hunted by limited permit only, and while populations are in excellent condition throughout their range, the chance to try for a bull in Montana, Wyoming, or Idaho is a rare opportunity indeed. Furthermore, the Rocky Mountain moose belongs to the narrowly distributed Shiras subspecies. While significantly smaller than its hulking northern cousins, a Shiras bull is a distinctive trophy and a unique challenge with the bow, especially for someone laboring under the cloud of a moose jinx as ominous as mine.

The wait for the results of Montana's permit hunt applications lends a strange edginess to the dog days of late summer. Every trip to the mail box arouses the stir of hope tempered by the statistical certainty that you probably aren't going to get anything good this year, any more than you did last year or the previous ten years. But one August afternoon the little envelopes from the Department of Fish, Wildlife, and Parks arrived, and there it was—right in the middle of my usual collection of mule deer doe tags and You Lose announcements: Valid for One Antlered Bull Moose. Never has blind luck been more deservingly bestowed.

The following day, my Shiras moose hunt began in earnest, not with archery practice or roadwork, but with a trip to the library. There are three North American big game animals commonly known by the eponym of the naturalist who first described them. While I had at least heard of Dall and Coues, I knew absolutely nothing about George Shiras. It just didn't seem right to try to collect one of his moose in such a state of ignorance.

In fact, Shiras turns out to have been quite a guy, a genuine New World Renaissance man who lived a life of remarkable accomplishment. Born in Pennsylvania in 1859, he became a noted jurist and legislator. His political accomplishments included the introduction of the first bill to place the management of migratory game birds under federal regulation. He was a respected amateur naturalist and wildlife photographer who pioneered the use of flash for taking pictures of game animals at night. All in all, he sounded very much like someone who deserved to have a moose named after him. Armed with this information, a cherished Montana moose permit, and a dozen carefully honed broadheads, I felt that I was finally ready to tackle my moose jinx again.

As hunting partner Dick LeBlond and I labored across the 9,500-foot contour line and set up our spike camp, I mentally reviewed the information I had obtained during a week of intelligence gathering prior to the actual hunt. I had spoken with wildlife biologists, game wardens, friends of friends who lived in my permit area, and a handful of people who had actually hunted there before. The conclusion was the same from all sources: lots of moose. *Beaucoup* moose. Moose all over the place.

I had my suspicions though. When a wildlife biologist tells you that a given location is crawling with whatever you are looking for, an alarm bell should go off in the back of your mind, just as it should when a Montana rancher concludes an incomprehensible set of directions by saying that you can't miss it. The terrain around our camp wasn't doing much to calm my fears. It was postcard-gorgeous scenery, but I found it difficult to visualize moose at an altitude generally reserved for sheep, goats, and light aircraft.

Once camp chores were complete, I parked myself on a log and looked back down the valley. That was where my instincts told me that the moose should be, but irregular swatches of blackened lodgepole pine crisscrossed the mountainsides like slowly healing wounds. This was the legacy of the 1988 fire season, a natural conflagration that consumed much of the Yellowstone ecosystem, choked the western states in smoke for nearly a month, and left the area in the grip of a management controversy that promised to take years to resolve. This was the big unknown alluded to by all my sources prior to the hunt, as one individual after another admitted that no one yet knew just what the burn had done to the area's wildlife resources.

I glanced back over my shoulder to see little dimples forming on the crystalline surface of the alpine lake beside our tent. There is no remedy for worry quite like rising trout. Within minutes after assembling my fly rod, I was admiring a vividly colored brookie that just happened to be the size of my frying pan. Ordinarily I release most of the trout I catch, but this remote lake was obviously choked with the rascals, and the choice between fresh brook trout and canned ham isn't much of a choice at all.

Brook trout it was. By the time the last of the light had faded from the basin and the oil was sizzling in the pan, memories of the moose jinx were all but forgotten.

In two days of hunting, I saw enough alpine scenery to fill a Swiss tour guide, a few blue grouse, and two cow moose. All remained undisturbed except for two of the blues, who wound up in my trusty skillet along with a day pack full of shaggy mane mushrooms. At least we had kept the ham in the can for another day.

Something just wasn't right. I know full well what moose sign looks like and the few old tracks and windblown droppings we had seen near timberline didn't fill the bill. "We need to go lower," I told Dick over lunch.

"Toward the burn?" he asked.

Well, why not. In Alaska, fires produce moose habitat. It's that simple. Mature coniferous forests don't provide high-quality browse. Of course, this was Montana, not Alaska, and last year's fires were so recent that the ashes hardly seemed cold. Still, all those alleged moose had to be somewhere.

"Toward the burn," I said, making an executive decision. "First thing in the morning."

And that is where we found them at next light, three bulls and a cow grazing together in a surreal landscape of darkened tree trunks. As I studied the moose through my glasses, however, I had to acknowledge the inaccuracy of my assumptions about the burn. This was not the study in desolation I had expected. Everywhere I looked, lush stands of new grass burst through the carpet of ash. Green and black were the only colors visible in all directions. The moose had clearly been more alert to the burn's possibilities than I had been.

I had already prepared myself for the fact that no Shiras moose was going to look very big by Alaska standards. Since Dick had been kind enough to put his own hunting agenda on hold in order to accompany me, I didn't feel that I could spend too much time being selective. I didn't want to shoot a mulligan, as year-and-a-half-old moose are known in the north, but I had already decided that I would settle for the first representative of the species to come my way. The largest of the three bulls made the grade. After a final wind check and a thumbs up signal to Dick, I set off into the eerie world of the burn.

It is important to note that the flattering review of moose that I offered earlier applies to the fifty weeks of the year when they are thinking about food more than each other. During the rut, the bull moose is a different animal. His bubbleheadedness makes a bugling elk look like a pillar of wisdom. A rutting bull moose can be belligerent to the point of becoming dangerous. When Teddy Roosevelt chose the bull moose as the symbol of his own feisty opposition party, he knew whereof he spoke. More than one bowhunter I know has concluded a moose-calling session from the top of a hastily climbed tree. Although the rut should have been easing into progress according to my own calendar, the bulls' tolerance of one another in the presence of a cow made it clear that they were still under the control of their brains rather than their hormones. I was going to have to do this the hard way.

I spent over an hour among the moose, never more than sixty yards from one of them and sometimes considerably closer. Had the bull that I wanted been alone or the mountain winds less capricious, there would have been no problem getting the shot. As it was, one set of eyes almost always seemed to be upon me, and whenever I managed to overcome that obstacle, the feather wind indicator on my bowstring faltered, sending me into a hasty retreat. Laced with dry, fallen pines, the burn was a stalker's nightmare. Echoes of the jinx began to whisper in the treacherous wind.

I did make some useful observations, however. The cow seemed to be the brains of this oddball outfit. Wherever she went, the bulls eventually followed, often matching her route step for step. Furthermore, the largest of the bulls was almost always the first in line behind the cow. It was time to borrow a basic move from the elk hunter's playbook. I continued to bide my time patiently, waiting for the right wind so that I could slip in behind the cow and set up an ambush. And that is exactly what I was trying to do when I found myself pinned down by the look.

After a full, timeless measure of waiting—waiting for the wind to arrive at the back of my neck and spoil everything, waiting for the cold, dark spirit of the jinx—the cow turned her head and wandered over the hill into a creek bottom. My left hand tightened on my longbow as the bull's antlers swung into view some thirty yards away. As I started to rise to my knees and draw, however, a warning light flashed somewhere in the electronic circuitry of my brain. From a bowhunter's perspective, a moose's front quarter might as well be armor plate. The bull's route of travel kept him angling ever so slightly toward me as he passed, and his chest never opened up for the certain kill. It just wasn't good enough.

They were three hundred yards down the creek bottom when I finally caught up to them again. Lulled by the warmth of the sun overhead, the two smaller bulls had bedded in a little alpine meadow. The cow was still feeding, while the bull I wanted seemed to be torn between an urge to follow her and the desire to flop down in the grass with his buddies.

After studying his choices for several minutes, he set off slowly after the cow. A small clump of brush stood well within bow range of the route the cow had taken. The wind felt steady in my face, and the grass in the meadow promised to dampen my footsteps. This was the tactical opportunity I had been waiting for all morning.

Monitoring the gaze of two sets of eyes, my progress across the open meadow seemed agonizingly slow. Somehow, I reached the brush before the bull passed by. As I watched his antlers weave toward me, I nocked an arrow and then he was there, right where he was supposed to be.

There was a time when I thought that being twenty-five yards away from a broadside, unspooked animal meant that the hunt was as good as over, but that was a long time ago. Years of experience have taught me differently. The bull was moving slowly enough to allow me time to take the mental steps necessary to avoid an embarrassing mistake. First I made the antlers disappear from my visual scan, for they are always the most distracting part of a trophy animal's anatomy. Then I did the same for the head and the neck and the legs, until nothing remained of the moose except a spot the size of a nickel behind the shoulder blade. Then I imagined the feel of the draw and the release and visualized the arrow in perfect flight, spiraling slowly through the air with the morning sun playing off its fletching until it hit the moose. And when I finally did draw and release, it all happened just that way, as if there were nowhere else in the universe that the arrow could have gone.

Mortally wounded, the bull spun and ran. His companions scattered, and then the meadow was empty except for the sunlight and the sound of the creek and the warm flush of my own excitement. I looked down at the delicate bow in my hand and marveled once again that an animal of such size could be brought down by an instrument weighing little more than the fly rod that had provided the first dinner of the trip.

Later, as we knelt beside the fallen bull, Dick asked if moose antlers always looked like this. I had to admit that they did not. I had noticed something odd about these antlers myself during the course of the long stalk, but I had not been able to define the quality that made them seem so unusual. As I studied them now, I realized that their peculiar quality came from their color. I have seen moose antlers flashing bone-white miles away on mountainsides. I have seen them colored pink, maroon, and scarlet as they emerged from velvet early in the fall. I have seen them in all shades of brown from tan to mahogany. But I had never seen antlers like these before, with every contour highlighted in rich chiaroscuro like a page from an artist's sketchbook.

When the explanation for this mystery finally dawned on me, it was as obvious as the charred surface of the log that I was sitting on. Fresh from velvet, the bull had been rubbing his antlers in the burn, and it was the great fire's legacy of ashes that had left its mark upon them.

And now, whenever I look at those antlers, I am reminded not just of the animal himself and the intricate conduct of the stalk that claimed him, but of the burn and how I failed to appreciate just what it had to offer. In terms of the 1988 fire season's final impact upon the ecosystem, the jury is still out. Almost everyone agrees that summer range for big game will benefit, but then summer range was never the problem there. Whatever the uncertainty, the bull from the burn taught me a valuable lesson: nature gives and nature takes away, and it is not always easy for fools like us to tell the difference.

The Prize

NO MATTER HOW much time you spend in Alaska, nothing can really prepare you for your first encounter with the North Slope.

The Arctic Ocean winds like a cold, gray snake between weathered headlands and the polar ice pack off shore. Navigable only for a few short weeks during the ephemeral northern summer, this must rank as one of the world's least hospitable bodies of water. Occasional native villages, oddly adorned by the clutter of modern technology, hunker down between the tundra and the sea like lunar landing sites. Inland, the Brooks Range adds to the sense of unreality as it rolls away in drainage after desolate drainage utterly devoid of the trees one expects to find in mountainous terrain. The Slope is above timberline, of course, by virtue of latitude rather than elevation.

From an airplane on a sunny day, the country looks deceptively for- giving. On the ground, one rapidly develops respect for all who live there. The area's few human residents are tough, or else they would be gone by now, or dead. The same can be said for the arctic fauna in all its forms: musk oxen, foxes, wolves, caribou, grizzlies, and Dall sheep.

It was the rams that finally lured me to the Slope some years ago, the rams and the opportunity to express my appreciation to my father for all the hunts he had taken me on when I was just a kid. While Alaska law stipulates that nonresidents cannot hunt sheep without a guide, as a first degree relative and resident of the state I could legally serve in that capacity. And so my father came north that August from Seattle, where I spent part of my own childhood and where he still works as a physician. I picked him up in Fairbanks and from there we flew north for that first encounter with the true Arctic in all its awesome wonder.

My trip planning owed a heavy debt to one of my regular Alaskan hunting partners who had bowhunted the area several times before with enviable success. He had kindly put some X's on my topo map to indicate landing sites and likely concentrations of rams. I noticed at once that the landing areas and the hunting spots were all on opposite sides of the river, which of course must remain nameless out of respect for his confidence. "Any problems getting across?" I remember asking once before our departure. He assured me that wading the river was the proverbial piece of cake.

But as we rattled to a stop on the gravel bar and the great emptiness rose around us, I wasn't quite so sure. It had been raining for days. The river was still clear enough for me to be able to see brightly colored char along the bottom, but it was far too high for us to wade. We hiked up and down the bank and checked several likely crossings, but there was no way to get to the other side without a long, cold swim. We could have done just that, but not without soaking and possibly losing our equipment. Only a blind optimist or a fool would begin an extended wilderness trip by getting all of his survival gear wet. After a lengthy strategy session over the map, we elected to proceed with plan B: a long hike upriver toward two drainages on our side that looked as if they might hold sheep. I have never regretted the decision not to risk the crossing.

Lowland arctic tundra is deceptive stuff. Because of the relative lack of the underbrush that infests southcentral Alaska, it looks easy to hike across. In fact, the uneven hummocks underfoot can be exhausting, especially with a heavy pack on your back. After caching some extra equipment and supplies near the airstrip, we began to arrange our packs. My suggestion that I carry an extra share went unheeded. Although in his late sixties at the time of this trip, my father is a former college athlete who always keeps himself in top condition. On our regular outings together, I kept waiting for the time when I had to slow down for him deliberately. The time had not come yet, and given the difficult terrain we found ourselves in, I hoped that this would not be the trip on which the years finally caught up with him.

As the guide, even if unofficial and unpaid, it was my job to worry about these things, but my concerns proved unfounded. We covered eight tough miles that afternoon before we finally pitched camp in a sheltered creek bottom, enjoyed a hot meal, and burrowed into our sleeping bags for what remained of the brief arctic night. Since he was still talking, I know he couldn't be any more tired than I was.

The following morning as I readied my equipment in anticipation of a full day of sheep hunting, I considered two unusual aspects of our hunting partnership. The first was the unstated reversal of roles between my father and me that had occurred slowly over the last few years. He always believed in introducing children to the outdoors at the earliest possible age, and I remembered well the hunting and fishing opportunities he had given me when I was young enough to have been a real burden. As my own skills matured, we then enjoyed the outdoors together as more or less equal partners for many years. Since my own move to Alaska, however, I had become the leader on our regular expeditions, and this trend had now reached a culmination of sorts here in the demanding environment of the North Slope. The responsibilities were obvious, and I found myself thinking of my own two children and my responsibilities to them as well.

The second unusual aspect of this hunt was the matter of having a rifle along in camp. I had hunted exclusively with the bow for some time and in the process had quietly parted company with almost all of my rifle hunting friends. Call it chauvinism or practicality; bowhunters tend to stick together, a fact that needs no apology.

We left camp under clear skies. With our full packs behind us, even the steeper terrain fell away easily beneath our feet. After several hours of climbing, we reached a ridgetop from which I could scout miles of sheep country with the spotting scope that I consider essential equipment for high country hunting. Unfortunately, we saw nothing but a few ewes and lambs.

As we rose to move on, I was startled to see a young male grizzly crest the rise barely sixty yards away from us. The bear spotted us immediately and rose to his hind legs for a better look. "No problem," I said as calmly as possible. "He just wants to see what we are." The wind was in our face, so I flapped my arms and shouted "Hey, bear!" or one of the equally ridiculous-sounding phrases that come to mind under such circumstances.

The grizzly responded to this fine display of Alaska know-how by dropping to all fours and running straight for us at full speed. It is difficult to appreciate just how fast grizzlies can move until you see one run toward you instead of making its usual retreat in the opposite direction. Fortunately for all concerned, the charge was nothing but bluff and curiosity. Forty yards away, the bear broke off and loped over the ridge in search of more excitement somewhere else.

"Interesting," I heard my father say in his usual understated fashion. He had dropped quietly to the rifleman's classic sitting position. His thumb rested lightly on the safety as the rifle's muzzle covered the hillside where the grizzly had just been standing. I remembered with private embarrassment my concerns about mixing bows with rifles on a hunting trip. Trust me when I tell you that a guy's father (and his rifle) never looked better.

As we came down off the mountain that night, I heard the rich, throaty chuckle of ptarmigan on the ground in front of us. Soon I could identify an oval head peeking up from the tundra. Eager for something better than a freeze-dried dinner as well as a chance to show my father what the bow could do, I nocked an arrow, picked a spot . . . and promptly sent the shaft over the nearest bird's back.

"Good thing that wasn't a full curl ram," Dad observed unnecessarily as the flock scattered and I began to search for my arrow. I could still hear ptarmigan calling from the creek bottom, and after digging my wayward shaft out of the lichen, I set off again. The birds cooperated, my aim improved, and an hour later we were roasting ptarmigan over a willow-twig fire while the arctic twilight faded all around us.

Our valley, it turned out, was full of grizzlies and ptarmigan, but it took several more days of hard hunting to locate the rams that we were after. Late one afternoon, after climbing to the very head of the basin, I swept the spotting scope down the next drainage, and there they were. As Dall sheep so often do, they simply appeared from the barren terrain as if by magic. To the serious hunter, there are few sights more compelling than the golden sweep of a Dall ram's horn, translucent in the sunlight. After watching them feed their way across the scree at the base of a rock face, I wriggled away from the spotting scope to let my father watch them while I planned a stalk.

Tactically, our problem was simple. The sheep were grazing over a mile away across rugged terrain, and most of our daylight was behind us. While neither ram was huge, they were both fine full curl representatives of the species, and each exceeded minimum standards for a first sheep for my father or a bow kill for myself. With that essential decision made, I began to outline an approach that would get us near the sheep.

"Have you looked at the weather?" Dad asked.

Not really; I had been too busy looking at sheep. Indeed, the wind was kicking up on the ridge, and the ceiling was dropping rapidly to the west. "Something is moving in," I agreed.

"If we set off after those sheep," he continued, "we're probably going to spend the night on the mountain without any shelter. I think that would be a mistake."

Quite honestly, I hadn't given the matter a lot of thought. I was accustomed to doing what you have to do in Alaska to get a shot at a trophy animal with a bow, and that sometimes means stretching prudence to the limit. Now I re-examined the weather and the steep terrain between our position and the sheep. As I did, I weighed my father's concerns. I could not reasonably expect him to do what I might have done, and fathers, as they say, know best. With no small sense of regret, I said my good-byes to the two rams and we started the long hike back toward camp.

My father's good judgment probably saved our lives. By midnight, the tent poles were straining against a gale-force wind. I slept fitfully at best. The following morning, my watch told me it was time to rise, but the inside of the tent was still shrouded in darkness. I crawled out of my sleeping bag and unzipped the tent fly to find an obvious explanation for this illusion. We were buried under two feet of wet snow.

The storm lasted for three days. The weather was so severe that we were confined to the little tent for its duration. Spending that length of time in the limited space provided by a five-pound backpack tent will challenge a guy's ability to get along with anyone. Fortunately, I was in good company. My father and I had been through enough of these sieges to make long paperback books a mandatory part of the wilderness equipment checklist. And so we read and listened to the wind howl and reminisced over four decades' worth of my experiences and seven of his. The time almost passed enjoyably—except when I stopped to think about what might happen if the storm didn't let up soon.

Although we did our best to keep the snow off the tent, the fly eventually iced up and stopped breathing. Inside, condensation began to seep its way into our sleeping bags. The scrub willow along the creek bottom was adequate fuel for a coffee-boiling fire, but that was about all even under the best of circumstances. If we got wet, we would never get dried out. It didn't take a lot of imagination to see that we were about to have real problems.

On the morning of the fourth day inside the tent, we awoke to the sound of silence. The wind had blown itself out at last. I scrambled outside to find a clear sky overhead and a warm sun beginning to assert itself in the east. Barely a hundred yards away, a blonde grizzly was digging ground squirrels out of the tundra in a great show of agility and effort. I don't know what the caloric value of a pika is, but it was hard to imagine that the bear was doing much better than breaking even.

We watched him for nearly an hour as we enjoyed our own first real meal in days. Once again, it seemed that the Arctic was meant for its survivors.

Sheep hunting, however, proved to be impossible. As a rule, one of the few easy things about hunting Dall sheep is spotting them. When out of bed and grazing, they stand out like golf balls on a putting green. A layer of fresh snow, however, will soon teach the hunter why a white coat is adaptive for so many species in the north. Furthermore, wet snow made the footing so treacherous that climbing became foolhardy. We tried our best, but finally gave up and trudged back down the river toward the airstrip, carrying nothing with us that hadn't been there on the way in—except memories.

It was a clear, gorgeous afternoon. Back at our cache, I dug out my fly rod and set out after the char that I had seen earlier, but they had all moved on upriver. Then I saw the caribou.

Hurrying back to camp, I set up the spotting scope and showed the herd to my father. There were over a hundred head milling about on the ridge above camp, including several mature bulls. "You can use your sheep tag for a caribou," I explained quickly. "Why don't you try for one?"

"Because I'd rather see you take one with your bow," he replied. "Besides," he added with a grin, "I'd rather watch you pack one off the mountain than do it myself."

I didn't need any more encouragement. I could not keep the caribou in sight during the climb because of the contour of the terrain. It took me an hour to reach the ridge where I had seen the herd, by which time, of course, they had disappeared. Veteran caribou hunters will not be surprised to learn that while I was going up one side of the hogback, they were going down the other. By the time I finally spotted them, they were trooping right through our camp.

After a good laugh at my own expense, I watched the caribou filter through the willows around our tent. A mature bull paused in the middle of the airstrip—as easy a game-packing job as Alaska is ever going to offer—and I waited for the sure crack of my father's rifle. It never came. Finally the herd quartered down the bank and into the river. I watched as they fought the surging current and eventually disappeared along their ancient migration trails on the other side.

"Hey!" I said when I finally made it back to camp. "Were you taking a nap down here or something?"

"Nope," Dad replied. "Just watching the show."

"The best bull in the herd was standing right in the middle of the strip!" I protested. "We could have taxied right up to him."

"I know," Dad said. "I had the crosshairs on his shoulder."

"Why didn't you shoot?" I asked.

"Well," he replied after a moment of reflection, "I had already decided that this trip has been one of the greatest experiences in my life. I tried to think how shooting that particular caribou was going to make it any better, and I couldn't come up with anything. So I just watched him swim the river instead."

And that is how the trip ended, with the trophies fixed in the mind rather than upon the wall and the best of friendships renewed once more by the spell of wild places.

On the morning of the last Monday in October some five years later, I chose to sleep in. That is an unusual decision for me during Montana's hunting season, but it had been a busy weekend, with duck blinds at dawn and tree stands in the evenings and all sorts of things in between. With a long week of work facing me, I had chosen to stockpile a few precious hours of sleep.

This sudden outburst of responsible behavior didn't do me much good, however. It was still pitch-dark when the phone rang. Through layers of sleep I recognized the voice on the other end of the line as that of another local physician, and I simply assumed that my work was starting a few hours ahead of schedule due to some emergency.

"Congratulations!" I finally heard him say.

"Thanks," I replied rather curtly. "For what?"

"You haven't been watching the news?"

I studied the clock face glowing in the darkness by the head of my bed. "No," I replied. "At five o'clock in the morning, I have not been watching the news."

"Well, get up and turn it on," the voice said. "Your father has just won the Nobel Prize in Medicine."

So began an exciting, hectic time for all of us. Because of the similarity of our names and the fact that I also have an M.D. after mine, I heard more from the press than I really cared to that week, although I was certainly happy to join in any tribute to my father and his work. More than one reporter asked, as reporters will, whether I saw any potential conflict between my father's lifesaving research in the field of bone marrow transplantation and his well-known interest in hunting. I certainly did not, and took great pains to explain why.

During one of our many telephone conversations that week, my Dad mentioned how that line of questioning kept coming up in his press conferences. He told me that he had tried to explain the value of outdoor sport within the structure of our own family, and the respect for wildlife and the environment that hunting had fostered in all three of us children. "I don't know," he concluded wistfully. "It's so hard to articulate. I don't feel that I handled it all that well."

"Sounds like you did just fine to me," I assured him.

"It's so hard to explain," he went on. "I wish I could have told them about some of the experiences we've had together over the years. I would like to tell people about one of those hunts, like the one in the Brooks Range, when no one even shot anything."

"Well, why don't you?" I asked.

"You're the writer in the family," he said. "Why don't you?"

So here we are.

It is a long way from where I sit right now to the Brooks Range. My father will probably never return, and it is possible that I won't either, although I don't like to think about such things. Everyone should experience the Arctic once for, having done so, the rest of the world will never quite seem the same.

Unfortunately, powerful forces are at work to rob us all of that opportunity. Driven by the usual combination of greed and money, these interests want to open environmentally sensitive areas in the arctic plain to development. Should this shortsighted attempt to profit from our country's lack of a cogent energy policy come to pass, the wild Arctic, real and imagined, will never be the same for any of us. Outnumbered and underfinanced, the opposition should have room for all who care, whether they choose to hunt sheep with a bow, a rifle, or a camera. Animal rights activists are trying to make such a coalition impossible, but then we have all heard far more than we want to from those quarters these days.

Amidst such discouraging thoughts, however, I still find the means to enjoy my own fragment of the Brooks Range, even if it exists only in the memory . . . the memory of the place itself and the company of a man who worked hard enough to accomplish another impossible dream without ever being too busy to take his own kids hunting.

Lascaux

ONE AUTUMN DAY on the eve of the Second World War, four local boys from the rural French community of Montignac followed a runaway puppy into a nondescript hole in the ground on the small estate of Lascaux, only to emerge later with fantastic tales of gigantic oxen, horses, and deer revealed by candlelight on the walls of their newly discovered cave. The fate of the lost dog is not recorded.

Subsequent exploration of the Lascaux cave by experts in all the disciplines interested in Stone Age man and his accomplishments confirmed the significance of the discovery. The cave mouth opened into a complex series of chambers whose dark stone walls bore marvelous images from a distant age. For anthropologists, this record offered new insights into the organization of primitive man's thinking. Paleontologists found a breathtaking eyewitness record of Pleistocene animal life that formed an unprecedented corollary to the study of fossil remains. The art community was amazed by the aesthetic quality of the work, and to this day every college student who enrolls in an art history survey course is likely to open a textbook on the first day of class to an image from the cave of Lascaux.

Beyond their general significance to the study of human culture, these paintings hold a special, personal fascination for me. In the first place, I define myself in large measure as a hunter, and from a hunter's perspective the cave paintings hold a special meaning that seems obscure to most of the disciplines that have tried to analyze them. Furthermore, these paintings represent the origins of what I shall refer to for want of a better term as outdoor writing. We in the business have fallen on hard times, and I can think of no better way to freshen one's outlook than to return to our historical source.

For the hunter, and particularly for the hunting writer interested in defining the significance of the hunt, there is no place quite like Lascaux. Let us now return there—to the wellspring of our species—and consider the lessons of the past.

To the geologist, the events depicted underground at Lascaux took place during the upper Pleistocene era. To the anthropologist, the times were late Paleolithic. What all this means in simple terms is that Lascaux's unknown artists spent a lot of time shivering in the dark because they lived during the end of the Ice Age, and chasing wild things with sticks and stones because bronze had not yet been invented. The consensus is that these paintings are around twenty thousand years old.

During the Pleistocene era, a series of glaciers advanced and retreated over what is now modern Europe. The accompanying fluctuations in climate and habitat determined the fauna present at any given latitude at any given time. During periods of heavy glaciation, the area was home to mammals clearly adapted to an arctic environment: wooly mammoths, cave bears, and ungulates nearly indistinguishable from *Rangifer tarandus,* the modern caribou. During cycles of glacial recession, the fauna were more representative of the subarctic steppe. With certain minor exceptions, the animals depicted at Lascaux belonged to this second category.

One of the most striking aspects of the Lascaux paintings is the degree to which animal life dominates the subject matter, a theme that recurs through almost all European cave art. The walls of the Lascaux cave contain two representations of plants. There is one bird. Only two human figures appear at all, and one of them, as we shall see, is having a very long day courtesy of an angry bison. The rest of the figures, nearly one hundred in all, depict large animals, game animals if you will.

Textbook reproductions of the Lascaux paintings inevitably fail to capture one important element of their visual impact: scale. The notion of a hastily scratched figure on the Ice Age equivalent of an outhouse wall doesn't begin to do justice to the proportion of the work. The largest of the bulls (*Bos primigenius*) in the cave's main chamber measures nearly sixteen feet in length.

Archaeological excavation of the cave's floor revealed a notable lack of the bones, fire rings, and other artifacts that were part of the daily routine of Paleolithic society. The only tools to be found were stone mortars of the sort that might be used to prepare pigment. Yet the position of some of the figures high on the cave walls indicates that their construction required the use of scaffolding.

Considered in perspective, the significance of these facts is clear. The work of the Lascaux artists was not casual. They deliberately entered the cave, which was separate from their living quarters, and subjected themselves to harsh, even terrifying, conditions for the sole purpose of painting. The artisans must have been supported by an organized tribal effort. What they were doing there was clearly very important to them, and what they were doing there was celebrating the hunted, *not* the hunter.

The Lascaux bestiary bears an odd, tangential relationship to contemporary animal life. Most of the subjects are ungulates. Horses, including some that bear an uncanny resemblance to the still extant Przwalski horse of the high Altai, were obviously a popular quarry, although modern hunters might have trouble identifying with that sentiment. On the other hand, there are red deer and ibex look-alikes whose horns would seem perfectly at home over my fireplace. The wild oxen bear an obvious resemblance to the fighting bulls of modern Spain. The final numerically important species is the bison, who appears as a wild and woolly precursor to the animal that so recently inhabited our own Great Plains. There are also a few exotics, animals that appear once or twice in the paintings and that were presumably unimportant from the standpoint of customary hunting activities: felines, a brown bear, a wonderfully drawn rhinoceros, and a strange figure near the cave's entrance of which no one can quite make sense.

Formal students of art have found all sorts of things to dither over during their analysis of these figures: the significance of the twisted perspective displayed in some of the horns and hooves, the relationship between pigment and engraving in certain figures in which the underlying rock was chipped to conform to the painting, and the peculiar spatial arrangements of the figures themselves, which in some cases overlap each other even when large adjoining segments of rock wall are vacant.

My own less sophisticated observations are from the simple perspective of a twentieth century outdoorsman. The animals are magnificent. The lines of the shoulders convey mass and bulk, reflecting the difficulty of penetrating the vital forequarter with a primitive weapon point. Indeed, it is the shoulders alone that occasionally border on exaggeration. The bulls are anatomically correct. The cows are sometimes heavy with young. There is no attempt to abstract the quarry from its own natural history or the need to interrupt it when hunter or tribe was hungry. Above all, the animals clearly commanded the artists' respect.

And what of the actual chase? As I have already pointed out, the Stone Age hunters themselves don't make much of an appearance, and yet Lascaux is still a hunter's tale.

A number of animals have clearly taken hits. In the so-called Nave section of the cave, for example, a mare carries a pair of missiles in her rump and a neighboring bison has been struck by no fewer than seven spears. Were the painters celebrating events that had happened or encouraging them to happen by the magic of their art? I don't know the answer, but it is clear even without the literal representation of the hunters themselves that the Lascaux fauna could not be separated from their status as quarry for those who portrayed them.

Of particular personal interest is the recurring appearance of small feathered shafts that bear an obvious resemblance to fletched arrows. As a bowhunter, I would love to believe that these objects are just that. Unfortunately, this is probably not the case. There are no bows portrayed at Lascaux. A wide body of archaeological evidence suggests that archery was a southern innovation that did not cross the Pyrenees into what is now France until nearly the time of the Bronze Age. The Lascaux paintings do show spear-throwing devices analogous to the New World *atlatl*. The shafts scattered everywhere were probably propelled by such devices rather than bows, but the fletching clearly foreshadows the eventual development of archery equipment as we now know it.

The early explorers of the Lascaux cave site required ropes and technical climbing equipment to reach the bottom of a long vertical shaft that descends from the cave's main chamber. There, to their surprise, they discovered the most narrative painted scene of all. This piece is unusual to begin with because it is one of the few instances in the annals of cave art that depicts a human figure. As a hunting story, it is so dramatic and immediate that it has few counterparts anywhere else in art or literature.

The composition's central figure is not the hunter but his quarry, an ominous-looking bison. The bull's head is lowered in anger. The hackles along his mane bristle and flare and his tail arcs upward over his flanks, all of which combine to suggest a mood of focused intensity. The reason for the bull's foul temper is obvious. A long shaft skewers his middle, but he has been hit too far back and loops of gut billow from the wound.

The object of the bull's malevolent stare is the clearest rendition of a human character in the entire cave. In contrast to the bison, the hunter is a mere stick figure. He lies supine, arms splayed and lifeless. A spear thrower, no doubt the one that launched the errant shaft, sits discarded at his side. The outline of a bird, the only one in the cave, perches nearby. Indeed, the hunter's own face is a birdlike caricature, perhaps even representing a mask.

Students of cave art have found much to question about this remarkable scene. Does the painting represent the record of an actual event, or an outcome that the artists tried to forestall through the use of magic? What is the significance of the bird figure, without precedent elsewhere in the cave? Why is there such a contrast between the graphic, marvelously rendered portrait of the bull and the childish caricature of his pursuer?

I can't provide any new answers, but anyone who has ever put an arrow into the wrong side of a large animal's midsection can empathize with the scene immediately. The hunter made a lousy shot and paid the ultimate price for his incompetence. *Hey,* the painting seems to declare, *we all need to practice more.* To his surviving companions who became the event's witnesses, the dead hunter looked trivial while the bull who killed him seemed to assume heroic stature and proportion. There is no attempt to clean up the record or manufacture excuses. In modern terms, one is reminded of Hemingway at his difficult best.

And so the art of Lascaux is unequivocally linked to the hunt. The subjects of these efforts are game animals, quarry first and foremost. The artists themselves were hunters, the product of a culture that defined itself according to the rules of the chase. Most remarkably, they were hunters who were willing to crawl into the deep, claustrophobic recesses of a cave guided only by some primitive form of a tallow candle just to record the majesty of the animal world around them.

Let us now fast forward across two hundred centuries of human experience and examine the lessons that the Lascaux paintings might hold for us.

The artists of Lascaux were not Neanderthal or Cro-Magnon human predecessors. The upper Pleistocene was populated by *Homo sapiens,* biologically indistinguishable from ourselves. And while twenty thousand years might seem like a long time, on the scale of developmental biology it is a blink of the proverbial eye. These people were just that: people, our immediate ancestors. The genetically determined instincts that governed their behavior were certainly quite similar to our own.

While hunting was obviously a central feature in Paleolithic man's daily experience, and a practically important one at that, other things were going on in the artists' lives as well: births, deaths, travels, interactions with other tribes, and the rudimentary grumblings of social organization. Yet none of these elements of Ice Age life earned a place on the walls of Lascaux. These people defined their relationship with the world around them through the hunt, and they are our own progenitors. Modern writers have struggled for centuries to define why man hunts. I find it expedient simply to look to the walls of Lascaux for an answer.

The cave paintings have an even more immediate significance for those of us who try to define the outdoor experience today, whether the medium is print, oil, or color film.

Successful practitioners of the form must come to terms with the need for someone, somehow, to sell things in order to justify their paychecks. Bowhunting literature is in a particularly sorry state, with all due respect to the few who write it well. Too much of our contemporary writing overemphasizes commercial aspects of the sport and dwells on technical solutions to difficulties best addressed in other ways. Too often the quality of the experience is reduced to arbitrary measurements and entries in record books. Above all, there is a disturbing tendency nowadays to glorify the hunter at the expense of the hunted, the conduct of the hunt, or the setting in which the hunt took place.

Contrast this catalog of shortcomings with the accomplishments of our anonymous, illiterate predecessors at Lascaux.

The focus of the cave paintings is always upon the animal. More cynical anthropologists have argued that these portrayals represent an attempt to ensure success during the hunt by gaining control over the quarry through magic. If so, the artists' motives could be seen as less than pure. But if this interpretation is correct, one has to wonder why the paintings of the animals are so beautiful. A schematic or even derivative portrayal would serve the purposes of the spell caster. The bulls and bison of Lascaux, however, are drawn with an elegance of line that any modern artist might view with admiration. The pigments are rich, often complex, and obviously represent the product of laborious effort. Romantic that I am, I cannot accept the idea that these figures were created just to help put meat on the table. Radiating awe and wonder, these paintings are a celebration of the *objects* of the chase.

The hunter himself is most conspicuous by his absence, and when he does appear it is only with great humility. These are not hero pictures. The Lascaux paintings suggest important standards that need to be acknowledged by modern practitioners of the art form. Above all, the hunter alone does not define the hunt.

It is a long way in space and time from Ice Age Europe to modern North America. This distance makes the Lascaux paintings' impact all the more remarkable, especially for those of us who have chosen voluntarily to hunt with traditional rather than modern weapons. Most contemporary games are contrivances played by arbitrary rules. When I string my bow and vanish into the woods, however, I am engaging in an activity that our distant ancestors not only engaged in themselves, but celebrated at considerable risk and discomfort.

When I find myself wondering why I spend so much time in the field and so much effort trying to record and define what goes on there, I only have to think of Lascaux.

The paintings make me feel that I am part of something, and I can imagine no higher purpose for art of any kind.

Chances with Wolves

THE UNDERGROWTH WAS thick and horrible the way it can only be in coastal Alaska. We started out trying to follow the high ground to the sea, but the brush and the lay of the land kept forcing us down into the creek bottom until we finally gave up and did what everything seemed to want us to do—walk right down the middle of the stream.

We were wearing waders; the problem was not one of getting wet, but one of getting there at all. The rocks that formed the stream bed were slick and sharp, and there was nothing to hang on to along the sides except devil's club. The fact that we did not know where we were going or whether there was anything there worth getting to was either depressing or inspirational, depending on one's point of view.

Finally, the water stopped flowing. The rocks underfoot grew slick with seaweed and the creek bed seemed to fall away beneath us. The water tasted brackish when you dipped your finger into it and ran it along your lips, and we knew that we had finally managed to reach the sea.

We had tables to tell us that the tide was falling and maps to point out that the heart of the tide flat stretched away from the creek's mouth toward the east. The devil's club was gone; it never thrives right at salt water. I reached up and grabbed an outstretched cedar limb and pulled myself up the bank. Now there was no undergrowth. A smooth carpet of ferns lay beneath the conifers, and I walked easily across it and broke out onto the edge of the tide flat, right where it was supposed to be. Maps, call me a believer.

The wind was light and treacherous. We were early, so we stopped and let the breeze shift its weight around. Finally we decided that the wind wanted to be behind us, from the west. After all the effort we had spent getting there, I didn't want to leave without looking at the flat, no matter how adverse the hunting conditions. So, we set out down the beach to take our chances and try to get the wind in our faces for the evening hunt back toward the creek mouth.

We split up with the understanding that we would meet at the rocky point that marked the farthest extent of the tide flat. Ray set off along the grassy channel of a little tributary stream and disappeared into the mouth of the forest, while I stayed out on the beach. With the sun still high and the wind at my back, I could not even pretend to be hunting, so I decided to go beachcombing instead. There is no such thing as a bad afternoon exploring a beach, no matter which way the wind is blowing.

I could see where the clam beds were by the lay of the beach and the distribution of shells along the high water line, but the coming low tide was not all that low and it was still two hours away. I could not get myself out of the hunter-gatherer mode, however, so I worked my way through the storm-tossed logs looking for bear sign. Huge glistening mounds of tarry dung littered the grass; I knew there would be a hunt if I could get downwind of the cover and wait long enough for the bears to appear, even if it meant hiking back out the tangled creek bed in the dark on a rising tide.

The first indication that something remarkable was afoot on the tide flat came from the mink. Mink are fascinating animals. I trapped them when I was a kid, and their intelligence and cunning taught me all kinds of things about the natural world even though I would now prefer to see the hide on the mink rather than in the guardianship of the furrier. They are secretive, nocturnal animals, and seeing one in the light of day is always special, the way seeing a grizzly or a wolverine is always special—no matter how many of them you have seen before.

I was standing on the edge of a circular cove, a piece of shoreline that would soon be under water. Nothing was happening any faster than the tide was coming in. Suddenly I heard footsteps in the gravel, and because I was thinking about bears, I looked for a bear to explain the sound.

The beach seemed empty. There was no bear; this much was obvious at first glance. For some time, there did not seem to be anything at all, and then I saw the mink across the water on the opposite side of the cove. There were two of them scrambling about in the gravel, and it was impossible to tell whether they were making love or war. They finally disengaged and set off around the edge of the cove in my direction with one fleeing wildly and the second in furious pursuit. I simply stood in place and watched as they approached. Although I was in plain sight on an open gravel beach, they seemed to ignore me completely as they drew nearer. Finally, they ran right across my boots and disappeared around the next outcropping of barnacled rock, leaving me alone on the empty beach. I have never seen mink act that way before or since.

The wind was shifting straight onshore, contaminating all the cover with my scent. I worked my way on down the beach toward the impassable confluence of rock and jungle that marked the end of the flat. Finally, I stopped at a tide pool to photograph a starfish so vividly orange that it seemed to demand the consumption of half a roll of film. The water was hauntingly clear and the light just right. There was no reason to hurry.

The tide was dead low by the time I finally reached the meeting spot we had agreed upon earlier. I put my bow down and selected a stick from the jumble along the high tide line. In a few minutes of scratching through the sand, I collected a dozen perfect, plump butter clams. I washed the clams off in another tide pool, and then I opened them with my hunting knife and ate them raw while I waited for Ray. At first I found myself longing for a lemon or a bottle of hot sauce, but then I relaxed and let myself taste the clams just as they were. I realized that shellfish did not get better than this, not in restaurants, not anywhere.

Ray showed up twenty minutes later. He had checked the second stream for steelhead and bear sign without finding either. We agreed that the wind was terrible, and that short of conceding defeat and leaving early, the only logical thing to do was wait and try to salvage a late-evening hunt. We would have to worry about the long hike back up the stream bed in the dark when the time came.

We were sitting on a log with our backs to the deep woods and our faces to the sea. I don't know what made me turn around, and did not realize until later that we had both turned and looked back toward the forest at the same time. Suddenly, a gray canine form appeared in a gap between the trees. "Coyote," Ray said. It did not occur to me to be surprised that I had seen it too, right there a hundred yards away, suspended in front of the underbrush like a ghost.

"Gotta predator call here somewhere," I said as I fumbled through my day pack. I was not doing this because I really believed I could call the animal into bow range, for predator calling is not one of my refined hunting skills. We were waiting, simply waiting, and there was nothing better to do with the time.

The call produced a harsh scream when I blew through it. Ostensibly the sound of a dying rabbit, it was above all else a sound that was difficult to ignore, like a baby's cry or the squeak of dry chalk on a blackboard. I called once, waited five minutes, and called again. The second time I let the squeals taper off as if they were part of a prolonged death on stage, a Shakespearean rabbit in desperate need of acting lessons. Then I forgot about the gray form back there in the woods and the predator call, and let myself settle into the last of the afternoon sun.

"Let's shoot some stumps," Ray finally suggested.

"All right," I replied. Whacking stumps with blunts is a great way to pass time, and I could certainly use the practice. I stretched and stood up, and when I turned around and looked behind the log, he was there—a mature gray wolf loping steadily toward us across the beach barely twenty-five yards away. Obviously intent on the source of the predator call's sound, the wolf skidded to a stop in the gravel. He stared at me briefly, then retreated with surprising indifference to the edge of the forest and disappeared into the gloom.

It is difficult to convey a sense of how startling this encounter was to me. There were wolves around my house, but I had never really met them, not like this. They left their tracks as calling cards and made the cold air ring on winter nights, but that was all impersonal. I did see wolves from the air from time to time, but those aerial sightings never really seemed to count. When I had seen wolves from the ground, the image was always distant and fleeting, insubstantial somehow, like our first sighting of the wolf that afternoon at the edge of the forest. This was different. The wolf had been right there in plain sight. He had been in bow range.

Suddenly, I realized that I still had the predator call in my pocket. Although the wolf had clearly seen us, I blew the call a third time. To my amazement, the gray form appeared again at the edge of the trees and disappeared into the jumble of driftwood at the upper edge of the beach.

"Get moving," I hissed. Ray, who had seen everything, scrambled down into a depression and crawled thirty yards forward where he took up a position behind a downed log. I flattened myself against the gravel on the open beach. Then Ray nocked an arrow and went on point, and I knew he could see the wolf again even though I could not.

We waited quietly, but I saw nothing and heard only the rise and fall of the waves at my back. Then Ray gave me a little hand signal like a conductor asking for more volume from an orchestra, and I blew the call again. Suddenly the gray canine head appeared above a log fifty yards from me and considerably closer to Ray. Although I could not begin to explain the call's nearly magical effect on the wolf, I blew it once more.

This time, the wolf seemed to make a commitment. Without hesitation, he started directly toward me. As he passed broadside to the log, Ray calmly and gracefully came to full draw. Then he calmly and gracefully sent the arrow whistling under the wolf's brisket. Later, he would offer a wonderful excuse for his miss. He still thought the animal was a coyote, and with no size reference on the open beach he had held as if he were shooting at a coyote at twenty yards instead of a wolf at thirty. At least that is what he said. Hey, world-class misses demand world-class excuses, especially when witnessed by one's hunting partner.

Whatever unusual mind frame possessed the wolf, it did not include having arrows tickle the hair on its chest. After Ray's shot, the animal retreated once again toward the security of the forest. I had been doing some thinking about the wolf's unusually aggressive response to the call. For an animal as secretive and wary as a mature wolf, something highly unusual was clearly taking place. I concluded that the call's effect could not be explained on the basis of dying rabbits, and that it must be evoking some sort of territorial response on the part of the wolf. With nothing to lose at this point, I decided to put my theory to the test.

Although I never expected to see the twice-spooked wolf again, I blew the call anyway. This time I added a deliberate lupine quaver to its crude melody. To my amazement, I was greeted immediately by a series of yips from the woods and then the wolf appeared once more. He had evidently learned something, because this time he refused to approach. Instead, he jumped onto a downed log a hundred yards away and began to howl.

This was real wolf music, the kind that makes the hair stand up on the nape of your neck no matter how much politically correct wolf drivel you have absorbed over the years. It is supposed to affect us like that; we are programmed that way. And that is what makes this sound so compelling, a point that is utterly lost upon those who would trivialize the wolf and reduce him to nothing but another version of the dog hero in a Disney movie. Wolves *are* predators—noble ones to be sure—but bone crunchers and hamstringers nonetheless. When one has something to say to you as this one did that afternoon, it is straight talk from one member of the Top of the Food Chain Club to another.

I howled at the wolf and the wolf howled back at me. He was not going to come any closer and I knew it. Ray was in a poor position to make a sneak but he tried anyway. I couldn't blame him. It was likely that no modern era archer had ever taken a wolf with a longbow. He did have the wind, but that was all that he had. Fifty yards short of the wolf, he reached a stalemate at the end of his natural cover. The wolf just kept howling, and so did I.

It is time for a candid admission. This is the sort of admission that is hard to make these days, now that the opportunity to do what we were doing is under attack from people who have never seen wolves, heard wolves, or been to places where there could possibly be any wolves. I make my admission anyway, well aware that it will be subject to misinterpretation.

I was glad that Ray had missed.

I never discussed this feeling with anyone, not even Ray. I did not mention my ambivalence about the fate of his arrow when I first told this story. It did not seem possible. The demands of the bow forge strong bonds, and hunters do not celebrate when their companions miss their mark. Nonetheless, I was glad the arrow wound up in the beach and not in the wolf.

My feelings had nothing to do with the politics of wolf management (more on this difficult subject to follow). Nor had I experienced some bizarre repolarization of values, the kind that shows up in movies that depict the hunters as bad guys while the film crew is burning the forest down for the sake of some award-winning footage. There was nothing that radical afoot. It was just that at this particular moment I was glad that this particular wolf was standing where he was, howling at me every time I howled at him. The wolf was reminding me why I was there in the large sense as well as the small, and I appreciated it. That's all.

Ray's stalk came to nothing. The spell was finally broken, as if everyone had awakened together from a dream. The wolf just stopped howling and stared at me briefly, and then he disappeared, leaving the empty beach and the sound of the waves where all had so recently been magic. Neither Ray nor I moved for some time. My silence had nothing to do with hunting or stalking. I just wanted the mood and the feeling of the place to gel, so I could fix it and conjure it up when I needed it. I knew even then that I would never spend another afternoon quite like this one.

All right: what about wolves?

Wolves arouse intense emotions from both poles in the ongoing argument over management of wildlife resources. Montana is currently embroiled in debate over the federal Wolf Recovery Program, a romantic but flawed effort to reintroduce the wolf to part of its historic range in Yellowstone Park. The idea has aroused intense animosity from ranching interests. Compared to the hazards of uncertain markets, high production costs, weather, interest rates, unsympathetic bankers, and agricultural politics, the threat posed to livestock by a handful of wolves seems minimal, but that isn't the way folks here see things. One crusty old ranch wife I know summarized the prevailing sentiment toward wolf recovery as follows: *Shoot, shovel, and shut up.*

On the other hand, I'll never forget the afternoon I wandered into a public meeting of the Alaska Board of Game to offer some testimony on a proposed archery moose season and found myself in the middle of a hearing on Alaska's aerial wolf hunting regulations. Even as a pilot, I happen to be philosophically opposed to the aerial hunting of anything, but I was completely unprepared for what I encountered. The room was packed with outside anti-hunting forces who had obviously incurred tremendous expense to get there. It was also obvious that they had no intention of stopping with the elimination of aerial wolf hunting. As I listened in numb fascination to several hours of their emotional and largely incoherent testimony before the board, I began to develop a sense of what hunters are up against in this country if we are to survive. It was a profoundly sobering and disturbing moment.

In fact, the wolf illustrates many of the problems inherent in the polarization of America's wildlife interests today. There is a broad, reasonable middle ground that is all too easy to ignore, and I would like to suggest it simply. Let's manage the wolf as a big game animal. No shooting from airplanes, no environmentally destructive poisons, no eradication programs for the benefit of moose and other more "desirable" species. And no pedestals either; throughout its Alaska range, the wolf is anything but an endangered species. Let's replace blind animosity with seasons and limits and fair chase. Let's replace hysteria with habitat protection and rational management. These ideas have worked wonders for every big game species in North America that has received their benefit. And for those who can't stand the thought of wolf tracks in the woods or wolf hides on the wall, just remember: that's your problem.

The two most elusive trophies in Alaska are the wolf and the wolverine. In the land of the grizzly and the wild sheep, that is a hard concept to get across, but it's true. As we walked across the tide flat that night to begin the long hike back upstream, we were both very much aware that Ray had blown a unique bowhunting opportunity. That was all right, however, in a way that missing a bull moose or a full curl ram is usually not all right. I could tell, because neither of us seemed disappointed.

I thought about the room full of people at the Board of Game meeting years earlier, people who had all kinds of opinions even though they had never seen a wolf in the wild or been to places wild enough to sustain them. In all fairness, I realized that I was glad our wolf was still out there, and I suspected Ray had similar, or at least ambivalent, feelings about his miss. Would I shoot another wolf if the opportunity arose? I would, if the circumstances were right and the situation met my own definition of fair chase. Of course, I might decline the shot as well; I would know when the time came. The real point was that I wanted the chance to decide the matter for myself. In order for that to happen, there must be wolves and wild places and the freedom and the will to go and enjoy them, no matter what the final decision about the shot might turn out to be. It does not seem too much to ask.

EIGHT

Bows, Arrows, and Dangerous Game

THE LARGEST OF the four bears using the tide flat, he stood out against the emerald spring grass like a glob of hot tar. Safely upwind, his coat glowed in the backlight from the evening sun as my binoculars confirmed the prime quality of his unrubbed hide. Judging bears is always difficult no matter how many of them you've studied, and I made myself come up with some hard estimates purely as a matter of interest: six plus feet, nineteen inches, three hundred pounds. Then one of his junior associates popped out of the brush across the flat, and with a second bear available for comparison I had no trouble confirming that the first one was a keeper. The stalk was on.

As shore birds turned in the sunlight overhead, I raced the incoming tide across the mouth of the flat. The wind—the usual bugaboo of stalks on Alaska's coastal shoreline—held steady in my face, and I closed easily within sixty yards of the bear. Of course, that is never the hard part. Finally, I stopped and slid out of my waders for quieter stalking. With black salt mud oozing between my toes, I slipped an arrow onto the string and set out to narrow the gap between us to bow range.

Soon I was close enough to hear the bear's jaws as he chewed on the flat's tender vegetable offerings. As he fed, his mouth opened and closed methodically, its lining oddly pale against the ebony-black frame of his head. He looked uneasy, with good reason. This was not his first rodeo. Two nights earlier, I had made a similar stalk on what I'm certain was the same bear, only to be undone when one of his smaller pals popped out of the brush unexpectedly, wandered downwind of my position, and spoiled the show when he smelled me and spooked. I wound up taking a hurried shot at marginal range for a well-deserved miss, and was still furious with myself for this breakdown in discipline. The previous evening, I had watched Ray close to within twenty yards of the same bear before things went sour. Tonight he wore the belligerent look of a bear who had finally grown tired of having bowhunters interrupt his dinner.

As I closed within thirty yards, he grazed his way down a tide gut and disappeared from sight. Near the edge of the dense forest, I sat down and waited, for if I have learned anything about stalking over the years it is that there is no substitute for giving the quarry an opportunity to come to you. All stalks end when one of the involved parties makes a mistake, and I preferred that the mistake come from the bear. Several minutes passed quietly. Just as I started to ease my way forward, I sensed something in the jungle to my right. I still can't define what I heard. It was simply a presence, like heavy breathing in a horror movie, but I knew the bear was there.

The logical explanation was that he had looped back through the cover and was about to emerge right in front of me to begin feeding again. Slowly, I eased myself into shooting position. Then the breeze shifted, quartering from the flat to the woods, and I heard the unmistakable sound of a bear's snort a mere fifteen yards away. *That's it,* I thought, suddenly crestfallen. *He's winded me and it's all over.*

But there were two things wrong with this glib explanation of events. The first was that I did not hear the chorus of snapping branches that inevitably accompanies a spooked bear fleeing through thick underbrush, a sound I was all too familiar with from botched stalks on this and many other hunts. The second was that the bear did not offer the surprised *whoof!* that usually heralds ursine alarm, but a slow, angry growl, virtually dripping with menace.

I was not carrying a gun, having decided some years earlier that firearms are nothing but a nuisance when trying to bowhunt bears. Ray was off at the other end of the flat somewhere, worrying about bears of his own. In short, I was alone and unarmed except for sticks and string, and I was also at point-blank range from that one rare bear who responds to human presence with belligerence rather than flight. *Interesting,* I thought as the hackles rose on the nape of my neck.

Then the bear pushed a small tree over just inside the woods. As I listened in numb fascination, he cut loose with a series of growls and started to tear the downed tree to pieces. The sound of thick branches yielding to powerful jaws rose from the edge of the cover. If this was meant to be a threat display, it was certainly an effective one. Interesting indeed.

I have gone through several phases in my own thinking about archery and dangerous game. There were times when the combination sounded like the definitive bowhunting experience and other times when it impressed me as more of a stunt. A perfectly placed bullet from a large-caliber modern rifle is capable of stopping any animal on earth in its tracks. A perfectly placed broadhead, on the other hand, even from the best of bows in the best of hands, is not reliably capable of stopping anything instantly—not a whitetail doe, not a javelina, not a coyote. Anyone who fails to appreciate this distinction needs to review how hunting arrows work before bowhunting anything, dangerous or otherwise.

What is dangerous game? If defined as an animal whose pursuit can lead to serious injury or death, the most dangerous game animal in North America is the whitetail deer. It's not that there is a new breed of killer bucks out there ready to gore and trample outdoorsmen, although once in a blue moon a careless hunter does manage to sustain a direct injury from a deer. I'm afraid that we ourselves are the problem, as usual. As long as bowhunters keep climbing into unsafe tree stands without safety belts and shooting at noises in the dark, people are going to keep getting hurt. Since the whitetail is far and away America's most popular game animal, it should come as no surprise to find that more people are injured hunting it than any other species. Sad but true, and totally unnecessary.

Change the statistic to reflect the number of hunters injured per number of hunters afield rather than the total number of casualties sustained and my own nominee for most dangerous quarry on the continent might still surprise you. In my own opinion, as well as that of a number of Alaska guides whose judgment I respect, the hands-down winner is the mountain goat. It's not that those little nine-inch horns are all that lethal, although there are well-documented instances of goats using them to defend themselves successfully against larger predators, including grizzlies. The fact is that hunting goats invariably demands travel into steep, dangerous terrain. On one ten-day trip in the Prince William Sound area, I made no fewer than six solemn promises to abandon goat hunting forever if only I got off the mountain alive. Of course I had my fingers crossed each time, but unless someone discovers a way to repeal the law of gravity, goat hunting will remain a profoundly dangerous sport.

Casualty figures aside, dangerous game is conventionally understood to imply an animal who has the means and the motive to do you bodily harm if only you will grant the opportunity. In North America, where most of us do most of our bowhunting, that leaves us with a fairly limited cast of characters.

Cougars, I suppose, are potential candidates for this short list. While no one spends a lot of time looking over his shoulder in cat country, any animal that regularly kills and eats two deer per week obviously has the physical capacity to hurt people. Of course, cougars are remarkably shy animals. After many years in lion country, I have seen a grand total of three other than those treed by hounds, and that is three more than most people I know. The one that I squealed in with a predator call certainly got my attention, however. And there has been a well-documented increase in serious cougar attacks on humans throughout the west recently, probably because expanding lion populations have forced young toms into more proximity with man than is good for them (or us). Certainly if all those "endangered" California lions are going to go on a feeding frenzy, I can think of some people who would make great additions to their menu. In the meantime, on balance, I don't think mountain lions really meet anyone's definition of dangerous game.

Which brings us to bears.

Are black bears dangerous game? My own answer is a qualified yes. On the one hand, I've blown *so* many stalks on *so* many black bears over the years only to see them bolt in panic at the first hint of human presence that it's hard for me to get too worked up about them. Then again, those same black bears somehow manage to injure more people in Alaska every year than grizzlies. And there is always that one bear in a hundred (or two hundred or five hundred—it really doesn't matter what the denominator is when it's happening to you) that seems to come with a built-in ornery streak, one of which we shall hear still more of later.

And so, in an admittedly subjective conclusion, it seems reasonable to accord the familiar black bear dangerous game status, at least if it is hunted by stalking to close range without firearm backup. Hunting from the relative security of a tree stand is another matter. In fact, the tree stand is probably more dangerous than the bear. Not everyone will agree with this opinion, but it's an honest assessment based on my own experience with the species.

Which brings us to the grizzly, about whom there is no such ambiguity. *Ursus arctos* makes everyone's list. Some years ago I read with interest a survey of professional zoo keepers who were asked what animal they regarded as the most dangerous to work with. The grizzly won in a walk. The character trait they cited most often in this assessment? Unpredictability. That's worth remembering in bear country.

Until I had the opportunity to hunt the wilderness of the Soviet Far East, most of my own close-range encounters with grizzlies took place when Alaska's bear season was closed, when I was armed with a fly rod instead of a longbow, or was otherwise not capable of turning the situation into a bear hunt. Nonetheless, such episodes left me with the distinct impression that being within bow range of a grizzly and being too close to a grizzly are pretty much the same thing.

My own best opportunity to take one with bow and arrow in Alaska came one October evening on the Kenai Peninsula. I had located a small stream with a late run of silver salmon that was easily accessible from my home, and it was no surprise to find that the bears, both black and grizzly, had discovered this late-season bounty as well. One crisp afternoon, I was hunting my way slowly down the stream when I heard a commotion in the water somewhere around the next bend. When I finally eased my way through the brush, I found not one but two grizzlies fishing busily just thirty yards away. They were both young bears, and for quite a while I told myself that the reason I turned down the shot was that they were just too small. There is some truth to this explanation, and it certainly sounds good. In fact, the situation was as follows: I was alone and once again unarmed except for my bow; no one knew where I was; and there was not one bear but two to worry about. As I crouched in the brush and watched them go about their business, I had trouble imaging anything my arrow could hit out there that wouldn't be a heartache. In short, I chickened out. I've reconsidered that decision many times, but if something doesn't feel like the right thing to do at the time, it almost never is.

A few other species warrant brief mention in a discussion of dangerous game. Polar bears unquestionably make the grade, but hunting opportunities are almost nonexistent. If the state of Alaska ever regains control of marine mammal management from the federal government, that may change, but I'm not holding my breath. Javelina look dangerous and are capable of great threat displays, but it's all show. Feral boar certainly can be dangerous, on the other hand. So can buffalo. Bison injure more people than bears do in Yellowstone Park these days, but legitimate buffalo hunting opportunities are so limited that it's difficult to get much of a feel for them as game animals. Alaska and Utah support the only free-ranging bison herds in the country, and the odds against obtaining a permit to hunt them are overwhelming. Besides, after all the controversy surrounding Montana's "hunt" for Yellowstone's surplus buffalo (to which bowhunters were not invited, by the way), I can't see the words *buffalo* and *hunt* in the same sentence without getting a headache.

Finally, there is the bull moose, a character whose potential belligerence during the rut should not be forgotten. A few days after hunting season closed one year, I called a big bull into my hay meadow for a photo session only to be sent up a tree in haste with lenses flying in all directions. While ptarmigan hunting, a friend once had to drop a charging bull with his shotgun at a range of five feet. Nonetheless, these are unusual events, and if we are to expand the scope of the discussion beyond bears, we'll have to change continents.

The opportunity to bowhunt dangerous game abroad is so narrow nowadays that one almost has to turn to the hunting literature for accurate impressions. I can't think of a better place to start than with the writing of the late Jim Corbett. I grew up with these stories as a child, and they were central to my own early development as a hunter. While Corbett didn't seem to have any interest in the bow, given the highly lethal nature of his quarry (he hunted man-eaters exclusively) and the human lives at stake, even the most chauvinistic bowhunter would have difficulty objecting. Corbett's skill at his craft, quiet harmony with his wild surroundings, and profound respect for the great cats that he hunted all exemplify hunting at its best. He would have made a tremendous bowhunter, and none of us should miss reading his stories.

Among modern era archers, several of the greats had notable encounters with dangerous game abroad, including Art Young, Fred Bear, and of course Howard Hill. Perhaps no one did it up, however, quite like a Texas attorney named Bill Negley.

In 1957, with a grand total of two bow-killed whitetails under his belt, Negley made a ten thousand-dollar bet that he could collect a bull elephant with archery tackle. On his first safari, he took not one bull but two, and then retired from bowhunting completely for a number of years. In 1965, he returned to Africa with the express purpose of taking the rest of the Big Five. His motives were largely competitive, since he wanted to turn the trick before Hill's protege, Bob Swinehart. (Negley had already dismissed the legendary Hill's claim to have taken the Big Five on the grounds that Hill's elephant had been wounded with a rifle prior to being shot with the bow. I have no personal knowledge of this controversy, and can only refer interested readers to Negley's book for his version of the story.) Furthermore, Negley searched his soul and decided that he wouldn't really be hunting dangerous game with the bow if he had a professional hunter standing behind him with a .458, so he banned back-up firearms from his stalks. For this I think even his critics would have to accord him a due measure of respect.

Before his obsession with the Big Five had run its course, Negley harvested a truly impressive collection of dangerous African game with the bow. He recounts these adventures quite ably in his book *Archer in Africa* (Amwell Press, 1989), which should also be required reading for any bowhunter with dangerous game ambitions. Written in a candid, no–nonsense style, the book is refreshingly free of the swagger that befouls so much modern safari writing. After all, how can you help but like a guy who cheerfully confesses to a clean ten–yard miss on a bull elephant?

Of course, there is a darker side to Negley's story. Vehicles were used a little too freely for my taste in the pursuit of game, although this was standard safari practice at the time. On several occasions, Negley describes an encounter with a rhino or an elephant as a fight, and all too often that is just what it became, with lots of arrows and long blood trails. It is clear that Negley was not a particularly good shot, and while his honesty is admirable, it's also a bit unsettling. Those who share my own conviction that a clean kill is the essence of the bowhunting experience may finish the book with reservations. In the end, I find Negley's story inspiring, although it leaves at least partly unanswered that central question: Should we be doing this?

Africa has been slow to warm to the modern resurgence of interest in bowhunting, for reasons that are a bit difficult to understand. Even countries that have legalized bowhunting for plains game have been reluctant to allow archers to pursue Big Five species. Regulations change constantly, however, and the trend toward more bowhunting opportunities on the Dark Continent seems favorable. If those of us fortunate enough to go there early represent the rest of us well, the future of African bowhunting should be bright. If not, we will be left with nothing but books and our imaginations to suggest what might have been possible.

What about the bad bear on the Alaska tide flat? I hope nobody really thought I would forget to finish a story as good as this one!

After listening to another minute of determined growling, I finally got a look at the bear when his head appeared through an opening in the brush scarcely fifteen yards away. Unfortunately, that was all that appeared, and a bear's head is certainly no target for an arrow. After staring me down for a moment, the bear disappeared, and once again I found myself doing what bowhunters do best—waiting.

I was crouched near the end of a huge old log that angled from the edge of the tide flat upwards into the woods. When next I saw the bear, he was on top of the log coming straight down it toward me, growling once more and making quick little feints in my direction. In retrospect,

I'm glad I wasn't carrying a firearm, for I might have used it. Less than twenty yards away and closing steadily, the bear was well within even my conservative bow range, but I had nothing to shoot at but forequarter. Since there was nothing else to do, I held my ground and waited.

Midway down the log, the bear finally turned enough to open up some rib cage. He was still quartering forward more than I liked, but I had been patient long enough and it was clearly time to do something. Since I couldn't think of a better option, I picked my spot and let the arrow fly. After the release, I noted two facts that improved my outlook considerably. The first was that my fletchings vanished completely at the exact point on the bear's side that I had visualized. The second was that at the moment of impact the bear turned and walked off in the opposite direction before disappearing into the growing shadows.

Time passed slowly around the campfire that night. At first light, Ray and I returned to the flat to search for the trail. Those who have not had the pleasure of tracking through coastal Alaska underbrush cannot really imagine what a hellish experience this can be; those who have can sympathize. It took us well over an hour to locate my arrow, which was lying completely intact thirty yards back in the jungle. That gave us the beginning of a faint but steady blood trail, and forty yards farther on I crawled around a log to find Ray sitting happily on my bear. The arrow had whistled through lung, liver, kidney, and great vessels in the upper abdomen before exiting completely through the opposite ham.

Does this unusual encounter mean that hunting black bears is comparable to pursuing dangerous African game? Of course not. I think the bear was simply being territorial and I doubt that he would have attacked. But he might have; we will never know. While skinning the bear, I found a deep wound on his face that probably came from a fight with another boar. An abscess extended into the bone under the eye, and it's possible that this injury had put him in his foul mood. At any rate, the episode serves as a reminder that even the most familiar species deserve our constant respect in the field.

And should we be doing this? Why not!

NINE

Spaciba, Katya

THE MORNING LIGHT opened above the Dzhugdzhur Mountains to reveal a riot of fall colors in the alpine tundra. After years of living in Alaska I thought I had seen the best, but these unbroken waves of orange, crimson, and magenta approached some sort of theoretical maximum on the warm end of the color spectrum. I was standing at the 3,500-meter level astride the belly of the great Asian land mass. Hypothetical raindrops falling on one side of the ridge would retrace my own route back toward the Sea of Okhotsk, while those falling on the other side would eventually reach the Arctic Ocean by way of the Lena.

I was searching for snow sheep, arguably the world's most majestic hooved animals. I suppose one could say that the project was not going well. For two days, I had been climbing mountains from dawn until dark with my friend Andrei Belyev, a vascular surgeon from Moscow, and long-time hunting partners Ray Stalmaster and Doug Borland. We had not even found a sheep track to show for our efforts. Since we were all hunting with longbows, the sheep would have been fairly safe even if we had managed to locate them. Even so, it was hard to feel sorry for myself. Our expedition to the farthest reaches of the vast Khabarovsk district had come off despite the tanks rumbling ominously through the streets of Moscow earlier that week. And then there was the small matter of the scenery, which was almost enough to make me forget about the sheep.

But not quite. After catching a few more breaths of rarified air, I shouldered my day pack and continued on up the ridge toward a basin that looked as if it should have "Sheep Crossing" signs posted around it. Not that there was much of anything to cross, since the nearest road was several hundred miles away.

I climbed at a comfortable rate for several hours. By the time I finally met Andrei at the head of the basin, clouds were moving in from the north. I had seen no snow sheep. He had seen no snow sheep. We might as well have been searching for snow leopards, or abominable snowmen. As we ate a meager lunch on the windswept ridge, the temperature started to plummet and I could virtually feel the dew point reaching out to grab us. I shot a few quick compass bearings, and after a brief conference we decided to drop off into the next drainage in an attempt to shorten the trip back to base camp. Then the weather engulfed us.

By the time we reached the tree line, we had descended below the clouds only to find ourselves hiking through wet, driving snow. We had not entered this drainage before, and it occurred to me that if I had miscalculated, we were in for a long, miserable night. Then I saw a totally unexpected plume of smoke rising from the creek bottom in front of us. It is always unsettling to find evidence of human presence in the wilderness when you believe that you are truly alone. Two days earlier, I had stumbled across the otherworldly ruins of a log building complex in the absolute middle of nowhere, and now I had been brought face to face with unequivocal evidence of someone cooking dinner. What kind of wilderness was this, anyway?

My usual response to such a discovery is to creep by as quietly as possible and go on my way. Now the terrain made it almost impossible to avoid the creek bottom, and I was certainly curious to see who else might be out here in the mountains with us. Besides, the smoke implied the presence of a heat source, which was more than welcome.

We were soon standing in front of a canvas-wall tent in a clearing that suggested Grendel's lair. Bones lay scattered about the ground in all directions. Horns, hides, and antlers hung from the trees along with a smattering of more conventional laundry. Acrid pine smoke billowed from a stovepipe jutting out of the wall tent's flank. An arc-tailed husky dragging a hand-hewn wooden hobble stood at the entrance. He looked friendly enough as he advanced toward us, but he also looked as if he could take a foot off if he wanted to. I was trying to decide whether to trust my well-developed dog charming ability or to retreat when the tent flaps parted, and there stood Katya.

A woman of absolutely indeterminate age, I could not tell at first glance whether she was closer to thirty or seventy. A broad smile almost disguised the jagged scar that ran from the corner of her right eye to her mouth. Visible below the rolled-up sleeve of a faded military fatigue jacket, her muscular left forearm bore the mark of an equally fierce wound. Both had been sutured by a surgeon who evidently felt that function was beauty, and who had never heard of a malpractice suit. From her right shoulder hung the Korean War vintage carbine that sprouts from every man, woman, and child in the Soviet bush like a fifth extremity. A pair of traditional amber earrings offered just the right counterpoint to her rugged appearance. In the dull light beneath the storm, the amber glowed with an intensity all its own. I had never seen quite such a combination of grace and durability in one face before.

Although she ushered us inside with a hospitable gesture that required no translation, I found myself grateful for Andrei and his Russian. He explained our presence while she prepared tea and offered us pan bread and red caviar from a salt-encrusted jar. The little sheepherder's stove warmed the tent to *banya* temperatures, and the floor was covered with reindeer hides. When I settled into their receptive texture I finally realized just how tired and cold I had become during our uncertain hike down the mountain. I was wondering about the propriety of removing my water-soaked boots and socks to dry my feet before the stove when Katya instructed me to do just that.

While the tea and food brought reluctant signs of life to my insides, Katya and Andrei conversed in Russian. She and her husband Slava were leaders of the native tribespeople responsible for the vast reindeer herds migrating through the mountains around us. This was their high country spike camp. She and Slava were directing the roundup of the last stragglers so they could begin their annual descent to lower terrain. There the deer would eventually be culled and processed for their meat and hides, as well as the antler products that provide rare hard currency for the region's desperate economy through the Asian traditional medicine markets.

Once it seemed that Andrei and I had been successfully revived, Katya rose and pulled on her boots. Slava was late, she explained, and she wanted to go look for him.

Where was he? I wondered aloud. Out there, she replied with a laugh, pointing beyond the tent flaps. If she knew where he was, she added, she wouldn't have to go look for him.

Setting out blindly to look for someone in those mountains during a snow storm seemed about as reasonable as renting a rowboat in Miami and heading to the Devil's Triangle to look for the Lost Squadron, but Katya seemed unphased. As she rose, she slammed a clip into the semiautomatic carbine and chambered a cartridge. What did she use the rifle for? I asked. *Medvyed,* she answered with a shrug. *Baronei.*

Bears and sheep. And how often did she shoot a sheep? I continued, remembering the ram's horns outside the tent and the paucity of sheep in the mountains. Katya giggled like a school girl and replied that she shot sheep whenever she wanted one. Perhaps, I thought, the mystery of the elusive rams had been solved.

Before she disappeared into the murk outside, Katya promised to visit us at our camp, and then she was gone.

The following afternoon, I returned from yet another fruitless day of hiking through the mountains to find a quartet of reindeer picketed next to our cook tent. Inside, Slava and one of his herders were smoking with Andrei and the rest of our Soviet friends. Slava had brought us a hindquarter from a freshly butchered reindeer. Katya thought we looked hungry, he explained. After accepting a dozen chocolate bars in return, Slava said that he and Katya would be happy to help us look for snow sheep if we wished. Then he and his companion slid rope halters onto two of the reindeer, hopped up between their sweeping antlers, and rode off into the sunset. I could not help remembering a familiar line from dozens of childhood Christmas eves: *When what to my wondering eyes did appear . . .*

The following morning, Ray and I hiked to our friends' tent where we found Slava waiting to help us search for snow sheep. After a quick cup of tea in front of the wood stove, we set off into the rugged terrain above their camp. I had been in reasonable physical condition to start with, and days of hard hiking had me nearly mountain tough. While I might have been ready for the mountains, I certainly wasn't ready for Slava. Despite the burden of his rifle, he used a walking stick as gracefully as anyone I have ever seen. He had only one forward velocity—fast—and like an airplane with a constant speed propeller it did not vary with the pitch of the terrain. Tobacco was the only thing that saved me. Whenever he got fifteen minutes ahead, Slava would stop for a smoke. The first ridge that we attacked was a four-cigarette climb, and we found no sheep on top. The second required six smokes to ascend, and again it was barren. Not to worry. Via my skeletal Russian and a lot of imaginative sign language, Slava assured me that the *next* mountain would be swarming with *baronei*. By the end of our sheepless day, I was so utterly exhausted that only a plate of hot reindeer stew saved me for the following morning.

We exchanged hospitality between our camps for the rest of the week. Katya brought us pan bread, red caviar, and wild mushrooms. We reciprocated with chocolate and gorp, which the reindeer herders loved, and instant coffee, which they did not. They were all fascinated by my only "medium-tech" camping gear. What was inside the orange lining of my down sleeping bag? Katya wondered one day. Feathers, I explained.

She and Slava exchanged worried looks. I had already learned that the natives depended on snow sheep hides to get them through the coldest weather outside Antarctica. And how would I survive the winter with such pathetic equipment? Katya asked.

For this, at least, I had an easy answer. I would survive the winter by going home.

Gradually, I learned more about Katya and the remarkable life she lead. Although Slava had once traveled to Moscow, Katya had never left the *taiga*. Self-educated, she read avidly; even their mobile spike camp was littered with books and magazines. She spoke at least three languages well. Like most of her people, she was a practicing Orthodox Christian. Soviet religious repression had evidently not had the stamina to reach this far into the bush. It was also obvious that Katya was a major decision maker in tribal affairs, a fact that is remarkable only because of the abysmal status women generally endure in Soviet society. During nightly radio communications with his other herders, Slava usually did the talking, but Katya told him what to say. I never observed the faintest suggestion of friction between the two of them.

One evening in front of the fire I asked about the ruined buildings I had found earlier in the week. Slava and Katya exchanged pained looks, and then the story unfolded.

The ruined cabins were a legacy of the *gulag*. During the Stalinist era, some ten thousand political prisoners had been brought to these mountains and abandoned to collect ore samples. If their output was deemed adequate, they were resupplied with food occasionally, although in the end they all starved. The KGB maintained as a standing offer to the native tribesmen a large cash reward for the right hand of any missing prisoner. The logic was impeccable. Survival on the taiga was nearly impossible for a healthy outsider. The loss of a hand was equivalent to a death sentence, and hands were easier to transport than bodies. Slava hastened to assure us that his people had taken no part in such affairs. In fact, the only known survivors were two escapees his tribe had sheltered at no small risk to themselves.

The wind sounded even colder than usual outside the tent that night, and for the first time since my arrival on the taiga I heard the wolves howl. The following day, I hiked back to the ruined cabins. Although I had not noticed it before, there were indeed unnatural piles of rock fragments hidden beneath the overgrown layers of moss. To say that man is a wolf to man suddenly seemed insulting to the wolves.

The following morning, Katya and Slava arrived in our camp just after sunrise. They were each leading a pack of reindeer and all their dogs were with them. Somehow I sensed a finality about this meeting.

Over tea, Katya explained through Andrei that Slava's mother had wandered off into the taiga, which is what the elderly people of their tribe do when they feel they have outlived their usefulness. Their base camp had notified them of her absence by radio the previous night, and now it was the family's obligation to find her remains for proper burial. Although perhaps slightly less ebullient than usual, Slava hardly seemed devastated by the news. What we seemed to be dealing with was nothing more than a dignified end to a life well lived. I remembered some of the ways the medical profession has required me to treat old women like Slava's mother who wanted nothing other than to die in peace. A long walk into the woods on a cold night didn't seem like such a cruel idea after all.

It was time to exchange gifts. I gave Slava my hunting knife and Katya a Leatherman® tool, with which I assured her she could fix anything. Slava opened one of the packs, and Katya presented me with a reindeer hide blanket elaborately embroidered with fur from a *medvyed*. They asked me to return and spend more time with them, and I promised that someday I would. Then they picked up their rifles and walking sticks, turned the reindeer loose, whistled to the huskies, and set off across the tundra.

While I am absolutely not a people photographer, I can now confess my longing to have captured Katya on film. The problem was that to photograph Katya would have been quite literally to capture her, and she would have none of it. I tried wielding the camera casually, but she always giggled and fled. I tried sneaking up on her, but she was too wary, and without saying anything she made me feel that I was betraying her trust. Finally, I did the only proper thing to do—I gave up.

And so my final portrait of Katya is nothing but the mental image of her waving back over her shoulder as she headed out of our camp that morning. She seemed as free as anyone I have ever known, and therein lay the final, wonderful irony. The same harsh qualities of the wilderness that made the taiga a prison without walls for Stalin's thousands allowed

Katya and her people unprecedented freedom within one of the most stodgily repressive societies of our time. There is a vital lesson here for all who care about the future of wild places.

And for that, Katya, that and the pan bread and the reindeer blanket; for all that and more, *spaciba*.

From the very bottom of my heart.

TEN

Russian Bears, Part 1: Close Encounters

THE SOUND OF a grizzly cub scrabbling up a tree is like the buzz of a rattle-snake: difficult to identify at first and hair-raising once you truly understand its implications. As usual, it all happened so suddenly. One minute Ray and I were hiking through the tamarack forest next to the surging salmon stream in peace, and then all hell seemed to break loose. The sound of the frantic yearling cub rose above the river's noise as Sergei, the Soviet woods-man and trapper who was introducing us to the area, pointed overhead, shouted in excited Russian, and pantomimed in universal sign language that we should draw our bows and shoot. Of course, that was the last thing we had in mind. At this early point in our exploratory trip through the wilderness of the Soviet Far East, my Russian vocabulary was strictly limited to the basics: *da, nyet, glasnost, perestroika,* and *vodka. Nyet* clearly seemed to be the best choice, and I was shouting it at Sergei as clearly as I knew how. Beside me, Ray was struggling with his twenty-five-year-old college Russian as he told the Soviets something that either meant "We wish to avoid the sow!" or "Your mother has bad breath!" What we had here, as Cool Hand Luke once observed, was a failure to communicate.

An hour earlier, Ray and I had listened to Doug Borland give our Russian friends a marvelous introductory lecture on the art and science of bowhunting. Doug is one of the dedicated Alaskans whose enthusiasm has been instrumental in the opening of the Soviet Far East to American outdoor interests. An old friend and long-time hunting companion, he had enlisted Ray and me to help explore bowhunting opportunities in this vast expanse of wilderness, as well as to help introduce native guides to the demands of the bow. With the help of our interpreter Andrei Belyev, a respected vascular surgeon from Moscow, Doug had spoken eloquently to our Russian team about the limitations of archery equipment and the special philosophy bowhunters bring to the chase. Everyone seemed to understand.

Evidently, everyone didn't. I've spent enough time in bear country to know that it holds few places less hospitable than the bottom of a tree containing an unhappy grizzly cub. As Ray continued his halting monolog, I knew that our cast of characters was about to increase by one, and that the new arrival was not going to be giving us a warm welcome to Mother Russia. Right on schedule, I heard a loud growl from the direction of the salmon stream. Brush began to break and then momma arrived, predictably mad as a hornet. As she tested the wind and searched for the source of her cub's anxiety, I tried to organize a slow retreat from the trees. Sergei finally realized that the *Amerikanskis* were not going to shoot a sow with cubs, but it was too late. The sow locked us in her angry gaze and charged. Ray and I were carrying nothing but longbows. I had already examined the Soviets' Korean War vintage military carbines and decided that they were woefully inadequate as bear stoppers. My initial concern that we might have to kill the sow was replaced by fear that she might get to kill one of us.

Fortunately, Sergei proved to be one cool customer. He put two quick rounds through the air over the sow's head and she hesitated. The cub chose this moment to scurry down out of the tree and disappear into the brush. That solved his mother's problem. We were soon hiking our way back to camp, and back to the drawing board. During the long post-mortem discussion of our nearly disastrous encounter, it became obvious that we were involved in a classical conflict of cultural values. As Sergei explained the Soviets' attitude toward the bears: "The *medvyed* are our enemies here on the taiga. They kill us and we kill them."

Clearly, we had some work to do if we were to pave the way for future American bowhunters.

As a former resident of Alaska, I never thought I would see a wilderness that could make our own forty-ninth state look small and tame, but I was wrong. The Soviet Far East (which is *not* referred to as Siberia by its inhabitants, incidentally) rolls away beyond the Bering Strait in a vast sequence of mountain ranges and river drainages whose extent challenges the very imagination. The area is a huge repository of fish and wildlife. Some big game species, such as moose, caribou, and the grizzly, are virtually identical to their Alaskan counterparts. They share a common biological origin dating back to the days of the Asian land bridge. Others, including the true Russian boar, the Siberian tiger, and the primitive musk deer, are as exotic as game animals get. Until recently, this was all academic to American outdoorsmen, since the area was virtually closed to outsiders. *Glasnost* and a desperate need for hard currency changed all that, and the imaginative efforts of pioneers like Doug have finally allowed the possibility of access by adventuresome American sportsmen.

Bowhunting, however, is still a brand-new concept. Doug had set forth the groundwork during many long, laborious conferences with his Soviet counterparts, but it was now up to us to show our plainly skeptical hosts how it is done.

While bowhunting for gizzly bears is never an easy proposition, this trip had gotten off to an anxious start even before our encounter with the sow. Three days prior to our scheduled departure, tanks rumbled into the streets of Moscow—and Khabarovsk, our initial destination in the country. The August coup resolved so quickly and favorably, however, that we were able to proceed as planned despite the anxiety of our friends and families at home. In fact, we could not have picked a more exhilarating time to travel to the Soviet Union, as people everywhere demonstrated feelings of hope unknown for generations, as well as truly heartwarming enthusiasm for all things American.

Now all we had to do was tackle those grizzlies.

The little tributary stream where we ran into the sow was literally stuffed with spawning dog salmon. The mud banks were solid bear tracks, and the remains of partially eaten fish lay everywhere. Despite the abundance of sign, several careful still hunts failed to produce any more bear encounters. Doug, Ray, and I all agreed that there were too many people along, and that we should ask the Soviets to stay behind while we hunted alone.

At lunch on the second day in camp, Doug explained our proposal. As soon as Andrei finished translating, Sergei, the most senior Soviet woodsman, picked up his plate, walked fifty yards across the sandbar, and sat down with his back toward us. I did not need a working knowledge of Russian to understand his response to being excluded from the hunting party.

"Doug," I said, "we're going to have another Russian revolution right here in bear camp if we let this stand." I walked over to Sergei, and with Andrei's help told him that I appreciated the way he had handled the sow without killing her, and that I would enjoy an opportunity to hunt across the river with him that evening while Ray and Doug returned to the spawning stream. Politically, it was the right thing to do, and I never regretted the decision.

For the next two days, Sergei walked me into the ground. Despite the language barrier, we established a definite understanding. He was fascinated by my archery equipment and shot up most of my supply of blunts. For my own part, I quickly realized that, despite our differences in background and philosophy, he was one of the finest natural hunters I have ever met. I decided that even if I did not take a bear, making Sergei understand why I wanted to hunt grizzlies with the bow was a worthy enough goal for the remainder of the trip.

The Indian summer weather was beautiful, and the scenery rivaled anything I have ever seen in Alaska. The river by our camp offered plenty of mid-day relaxation with the fly rod, as it was teeming with salmon, Arctic char, grayling, and *kundzha,* an exotic char that provided tremendous light tackle opportunities. I even arrowed a ruffed grouse dinner, but the big bears remained elusive, and Doug finally summoned the helicopter to move our camp to another area.

The following afternoon we returned to the isolated village that served as our base of operations to pick up Andrei Shepin, the district's senior sable trapper and Doug's principal contact in the area. It was obvious that Andrei was every bit as capable as Sergei and the rest of our team. We then flew across another expanse of wilderness and landed on a remote river where the pilot assured us he had recently seen large numbers of bears. Unfortunately, his information was several weeks old, and the salmon run that had lured the grizzlies to the river in the first place was over. While we were disappointed to find ourselves on an empty salmon stream with nothing but old bear sign, we knew that there were fish below us somewhere. After a brief war council, we decided upon an ambitious plan. Early the next morning, Andrei Belyev and Peter, our cook, loaded a skeleton camp into two tiny inflatable rafts, and we set out to hunt our way downstream to the fish . . . and the grizzlies that we knew were feeding on them.

Two days and thirty long miles later, we began to run into the decaying remains of the river's pink salmon run. The bear sign grew fresher at once, and we began to hunt with the special level of intensity reserved for dangerous game.

That afternoon, Sergei and I were trying to pick our way around a cliff next to the river when we saw Ray, Doug, and Andrei Shepin crouch down suddenly on the opposite bank. Soon I could see a mature grizzly lumbering up the gravel bar in front of them. The bear was moving downwind, the bar was only fifteen yards wide, and it was immediately apparent that the grizzly was going to close within bow range soon. I watched Ray pull an arrow from his quiver as the grizzly disappeared behind a fold in the river bank. Long seconds ticked by. Suddenly, I saw the bear's massive shoulder hump swing into view, looming over Ray. The urge to shout a warning was almost overwhelming. In fact, Ray had been in excellent bow range of the bear the entire time. The approaching animal had simply never turned to give him the necessary broadside. Finally, he had to do something, and to his credit he elected to try to draw his bow and get off a shot as the bear walked by. For better or worse, the bruin saw the movement, gave him a hard stare, and bolted back into the cover before he could shoot. After Sergei and I forded the river and replayed the encounter with our hunting partners, we determined that the bear had been eight feet from Ray when he tried to draw. That, my friend, is just too close!

We discussed this white-knuckle episode again and again around the campfire that night. I had no doubt that many archers would have chanced the quartering forward shot as the bear approached, but I commended Ray on his remarkable restraint. We have both had plenty of experience with arrows and bears, and we knew that nothing less than a perfect shot would do, especially since our quarry was the most formidable animal in the northern hemisphere and we were serving as ambassadors for the sport of bowhunting. As Ray himself so aptly put it, "A grizzly is going to have to *ask* for my arrow before I take a shot!" I agreed completely, certain that it was only a matter of time until I found myself in the same situation. In fact, my turn to face the challenge of the Russian bear came two days later, on the final morning of our trip.

A cool mist hung over the river as we set out, and the air was heavy with the smell of decaying fish. Barely an hour out of camp, Sergei and I suddenly caught a glimpse of a grizzly coming toward us through the scrub willow along the riverbank. Once again, the bear was moving downwind, and the narrow bank virtually guaranteed a close encounter of some kind. Sergei, who seemed to have gotten a better look at the rapidly advancing bear than I had, was trying to tell me something that I could not understand. Once again communication problems took their toll. "*Medvyed,*" I whispered in my minimally improved Russian. "*Bolshoi?*"

Sergei shrugged noncommittally. No, he did not think it was a big bear. When he held out three fingers insistently, I concluded that he thought it was a sow with twin cubs and indicated that I did not wish to shoot it. This left us with the problem of what to do with the bear, which was in the process of walking into our laps. As I watched the grizzly approach through the willows, I noted that the bear was plenty large enough for me, and I had yet to see a cub. Suddenly realizing that something didn't add up, I nocked an arrow and dropped to one knee just as the bear rounded the last of the willows a mere dozen yards away. With nary a cub in sight, I was in the process of picking a spot on the bear's side when he fixed us in his myopic stare and took two quick steps forward. Sergei, who in fact had been trying to tell me that he thought our bear looked like a three-year-old boar, decided that this was quite close enough for a grizzly he didn't think I wanted to shoot. Logically enough, he rose and thrust the muzzle of his little carbine into the bear's face. From point-blank range, the grizzly stared at us for several of the longest seconds of my life, then vanished back into the brush.

It took Sergei and I several minutes of elaborate sign language to explain to each other our own versions of events and decipher what had happened, at which point there was nothing to do but share the international language of relieved laughter. The morning, however, was not over yet.

Less than a mile farther upriver, we spotted a second bear dredging salmon carcasses up from the river bottom. A solitary male, there was no doubt about his suitability as a trophy. We closed easily to fifty yards before we ran out of cover. The next move was up to the bear.

Rather than continuing on down the bank into bow range, however, our quarry finally turned and disappeared into the brush in front of us. The wind held, and so did I. Soon I could distinguish a dark form ahead of me in the alders. Less than fifteen yards away, the huge bear stood on his hind legs and proceeded to scratch his back leisurely against a tree trunk. The range was right and there was plenty of vital area to shoot at, but this time there was simply too much brush between us.

As the bear rolled and scratched almost literally under my nose, I slid an arrow onto my bowstring and tried to review my options. The usual solution to bowhunting problems is to try to get closer, but I was already more than close enough. If the bear passed between my position and the river, I would have an open shot, but it if he continued on through the woods he would remain screened by thick brush. Finally I identified a narrow shooting lane and determined that if the bear continued in that direction I would have to hope that he passed through it.

The bear stopped grooming himself at last and began to move. As he approached the little gap in the brush, I came to full draw. Suddenly, the shooting lane was full of bear. Just as I was about to release, the fail-safe light flashed its warning in my brain. Things were happening too fast. I could not be absolutely certain of my target even though it was only a few paces away. I have always been fascinated by the analogies between bowhunting and bullfighting. I knew in my heart that to release the arrow would be to take an amateurish swipe at an opponent that deserved better. In short, the grizzly did not ask for my arrow, and I did not give it to him.

Any endeavor as ambitious as taking a grizzly with a longbow requires a will to succeed, and I would be dishonest if I pretended not to wish I had come home from Russia with a bear. However, it is also difficult to write this off as an unsuccessful trip, not with all that fantastic country visited and all those new friendships forged. I had learned important things about my own ability to function as a predator at point-blank range from grizzlies, and in the end I knew I made the right decisions when it was all on the line.

Furthermore, I was satisfied that we had given the Soviet woodsmen an honest introduction to the way of the bow, which demands above all else an odd marriage of enthusiasm and restraint. The night before the helicopter arrived to pick us up at the end of our march to the sea, we drank the last of the vodka and talked about the bears until Andrei Belyev couldn't stand to translate any more. The Soviets invited us to return again next spring to take up the track of the grizzly where we had left off, and we agreed that we would.

Talk about an offer you can't refuse.

ELEVEN

Russian Bears, Part 2: And Nothing But the Truth

The writer has attempted to write an absolutely true book to see whether the shape of a country and the pattern of a month's action can, if truly presented, compete with a work of the imagination.

Ernest Hemingway, *Green Hills of Africa*

ALTHOUGH I HAVE no more reliable companion in the field, Ray Stalmaster is my sternest critic when I write. Simply put, Ray does not care for my writing, which has bothered me for years. We both read avidly and share most tastes in literature. Since we get along well under even the most trying conditions in the outdoors, I always expected Ray to enjoy what I write. This has not been the case.

At first I thought his lack of enthusiasm simply reflected a generic dislike for outdoor writers. I happen to know he places them somewhere between unscrupulous lawyers and animal rights activists on the short mental list we all keep of people we would not care to share a cabin with during a long winter. To tell you the truth, I can empathize with that opinion. However, his indifference has deeper roots.

For a while I thought that Ray was afraid I would reveal the locations of some of the special places where we hunt and fish. That is not a groundless concern, since revealing other people's secrets is one of the surest pathways to success in the outdoor writing business. But after years of "Somewhere in the wilds of Alaska . . ." stories, I felt I had offered adequate assurance that my own solitude was more important to me than seeing my name in print.

Finally Ray confided in me. My problem was born in 1899. My problem had a beard and disliked his mother. My problem was the same problem that haunts every American male who writes about the outdoors in complete sentences. My problem, according to Ray, was Ernest Hemingway, in comparison to whom I suffer greatly.

Well, *mea culpa*. My admiration for Hemingway stops well short of reverence. It is my opinion that his output as a writer consisted of one masterpiece of a novella, a dozen excellent and a number of good short stories, two solid novels, some fine, politically incorrect Africana, the definitive English-language discussion of bullfighting, and a remarkable amount of crap, much of the latter, in all fairness, published after the writer's death. (Comparisons of this body of work to my own are not invited.) There is ample evidence from his own writing to convince me that Hemingway, as a sportsman, would be on my own list of people I would rather not have in my canoe during a long wilderness trip. All in all, I can enjoy Papa at his best and leave him the other 70 percent of the time.

Ray, on the other hand, approaches Hemingway with fundamentalist zeal. The most affected examples of Hemingway's prose style leave Ray numb with admiration. Everything the man ever did was good and true . . . oh, hell. You get the picture. And in Ray's mind, the truest credo in all outdoor writing comes at the beginning of *Green Hills of Africa,* when the author announces his intention to tell the story of the safari exactly and literally as it happened. And therein lies the heart of the matter, for, you see, I do not always tell the truth.

I want to be very clear about the meaning of that last statement, lest my reputation suffer irreparable harm and all my readers give up on me forever. If I say that I shot something, I shot it. If I say that I killed it with one well-placed arrow, I did. To offer less than the literal truth in print about such matters would be, well, to lie. We can't have that.

On the other hand, if it improves the flow of the narrative to say that something that happened on the third day of a hunt happened on the fifth day instead, I have no problem doing so, as long as no issues of substance are involved. If I want to burn a paragraph describing a sunset that really wasn't much to look at, that's my business. Maybe that is just the way I saw things that night. I regard the suggestion of possibilities as part of my job description. Call it poetic license if you will.

For Ray, this is not good enough, and since he is about as likely to change his mind as one of his Chesapeake Bay retrievers, it never will be. Never mind that the literal description of events can make tedious reading, and that such renditions are better suited to the operators of video cameras than to real writers with adjectives and similes and such at their fingertips.

It is May 1992. Ray and I are about to make our second trip to the Soviet Far East to bowhunt grizzlies, renew some important friendships, and, with luck, finish what we started the previous August. And I make this promise in advance. This one is for you, Ray. This one is for Hemingway's ghost. From now until our return, consider my poetic license revoked. For better or for worse, the account of this hunt will be the truth, the whole truth, and nothing but the truth. So help me God.

This has been billed as a spring bear hunt. Spring is supposed to be the season of renewal here in the Far North, a fact that is difficult to keep in mind during our helicopter ride down the wild North Pacific shoreline.

As a former Alaskan pilot, I should be used to this sort of thing, but we are pushing judgment to the limit. The ceiling is indefinite, the visibility a half-mile in blowing snow. During the first leg of the flight, there is no terrain to deal with as nothing but flat beach glides by underneath. The pilot always has the old scud runner's option of making a wide turn over the ocean, establishing a controlled descent until he sees something, and then groping his way back to something else. We can live with that.

But then we reach the headlands, great weathered outcroppings of rock that intrude their way into the storm-tossed sea. New measures of turbulence seem to wait around every bend. Clouds of nesting sea birds erupt from the cliffs as we pass, screaming silently beyond the helicopter's windows at our unexpected intrusion into their lonely world. By even the most reasonable standards, our flight has become some sort of descent into hell.

One considers strange problems in situations such as this. I find myself remembering the last American woman I talked to, perhaps because of the possibility that she will be the last American woman I ever talk to.

This strange encounter took place the previous day as we arrived in country. The Khabarovsk airport stands as an elaborate metaphor for all that is wrong with the remains of the former Soviet Union. For years, Aeroflot enjoyed the distinction of being one of the few Soviet institutions that actually worked. Now idle aircraft line the tarmac in all directions. Even though the pilots still maintain their crisp edge of professionalism, they wear the grim air of resignation appropriate to officers aboard a sinking ship.

The airport terminal is a case study in illogic. Everything requires permits. Obtaining permits requires standing in lines that may or may not lead to the permit one is seeking. All lines intersect randomly, forcing everyone to become jostling adversaries in the attempt to accomplish the simplest of goals. Getting one's self and gear from an arriving aircraft through customs can become an exercise in despair. Because I had previously been through this on our first trip to the region, however, I felt like a seasoned veteran.

As I waited idly, an earnest young woman approached. There could be no doubt about her nationality. She wondered what had gone wrong with our luggage.

"Nothing," I told her. "We're in Russia."

"And why are you here?" she asked.

I considered telling her that I was a writer and a photographer, but that would only have postponed the inevitable reckoning. "I am bowhunting grizzly bears," I said.

Her engaging expression faded. "And what do you plan to do with one if you catch it?" she demanded.

I noted her regrettable choice of verb uneasily. "I will honor the bear's spirit every day for the rest of my life," I replied. This was the best I could do. Our conversation was over. She turned and disappeared into the crowd, and I went back to the mindless business of waiting.

Now as our helicopter yaws its way around another corner in the coastline, I reconsider this exchange. Perhaps I made too much of it. It also seems possible that by attempting to explain something I love to someone who did not understand, I managed to define some of my own reasons for being here. To honor the bear's spirit: I will remember this in the days to come.

For we know that there are bears waiting for us down there in the murk, and few people know more about them than my friend Andrei Shepin, who is now sitting beside me on the pile of gear stuffed into the helicopter's belly. Andrei reminds me physically of a wolverine. He is compact, muscular, and seemingly immune to fatigue. A broad smile appears upon his weathered face at the slightest opportunity. He is also someone you would prefer to have on your side in a fight.

Above the roar of the helicopter's engine, Andrei and I are trying to renew the friendship we established the previous year. Noise and the language barrier make this a challenge. Despite my reasonable ear for other tongues and my nearly month-long stay here the previous summer, my Russian includes only the most basic of basics. I can identify game animals and order a drink. I can name the Pacific salmon species, say good morning, and express enthusiasm and dismay. Andrei's English is comparable to my Russian, and we must rely once again on help from Andrei Belyev, the only bilingual member of our party, to communicate all but the simplest ideas. I am disappointed that Sergei could not join us this spring, but Ivan, his replacement, is obviously personable and capable. I am happy with the composition of our crew.

There has been mention of snow during the week preceding our second trip. As we turn upriver into the teeth of the country, the landscape becomes solid white. When we reach camp at last, the pilot can only hover above what was once a gravel bar as we pitch our equipment and finally ourselves out into the soup. Then the helicopter abandons us, and there is nothing to do but haul our gear through the drifts to the tents pitched in the trees. There we meet Victor, the camp cook, who, we will soon discover, exhibits an unfortunate reciprocal relationship between vodka and folk music. As more of the former goes in, more of the latter comes out.

An hour later I am standing on an ice ledge along the river, attempting to stem the rising tide of despair with an instrument ideally suited to the purpose: my fly rod. The Russians answered with an emphatic *nyet* when we asked about fish in the river, but I have never yet found water in this country that didn't hold something worth catching. This time the something turns out to be bright anadromous char weighing up to six pounds.

A Russian friend once told me that the Khabarovsk street urchins identify Americans in the passing crowds by noting the look of optimism on their faces. Now that we optimists have shown up the Russians with our fly rods, there is nothing left for us to do but find a way to hunt grizzlies in chest-deep snow.

I have spent two hours this morning working my way along the ice ledges that line the river with Ivan and Pat Barker, the third American member of our party. The air is warming all around us in the sun, turning the hip-deep snow into layers of white glue. We have seen fox and wolf sign, but there has been no evidence of *medvyed*.

Now, suddenly, there are bear tracks underfoot. Through my glasses, I can retrace the bear's route down off the mountain through the fresh snow. Here his way intersects our own only to disappear into a tangle of brush separating us from a distant bend in the river, where I can now imagine him rooting through the ice for salmon carcasses. Because of a tricky wind, there is nothing to do but cut through the swamp and try to work back upstream toward the bear.

Snowshoeing is a lost art for the most part, and one that I'm never sure I found in the first place—even under the best of conditions. Now we are working our way through a brush tangle on the shoes we made last night from saplings, rawhide, and burlap potato sacks. The snow is wet and heavy, and it congeals upon the burlap with every step.

When we finally emerge two hours later downstream and down-wind of the spot where I expect the bear to be, we are utterly exhausted. The banks are barren except for the rotting carcasses of last year's fish. With my glasses, I can pick out the bear's track again, and follow it from the river, up the mountain, and out of our lives.

The wind switches. Exhausted, we must work our way home futilely with the breeze at the back of our necks. I wonder if the Khabarovsk street kids would be able to pick me out of the crowd now.

After four more days fighting the snow, we call for an evacuation and move our camp downstream toward the sea. Andrei has it in his head that the bears will be on the hillsides, while I remain convinced that the only reasonable place to hunt them is on the beach, where we can maneuver with some degree of freedom. We try the ridge above our new camp, but it is no good because of the snow, and after an early dinner, four of us set off to scout a route to the sea.

Imagine alders studded with hypodermic needles and you will have a good fix on *slanek,* a diabolically designed low bush conifer that inhabits the region's lower elevations. It seems designed for no purpose other than to hide bears and impede human progress. After fighting the stuff for an hour, we emerge onto an open coastal plain. A broad gravel beach and the Sea of Okhotsk are right there in front of us at last. We can walk and we can see. This feels like some sort of resurrection.

The junction of the flooded river and the ocean is a cauldron of activity, with ducks and sea birds wheeling above the surf. After days of frustration, I am content to sit down on a log with my glasses and relax, studying the action and trying to fill in a few tenacious blanks in my life list of waterfowl with some of the smews and pochards that have eluded me over the years. Then the bear appears.

At first he is nothing but a black dot a mile away on the beach, but his lumbering grizzly-bear gait is apparent even at this distance. After winning a coin toss with Ray, Andrei and I set off down the bluff while Ray and Ivan settle in behind a log to watch the show.

It is difficult to feel confident. I have a quartering wind to work with at best, there is no cover at all upon the beach, and the bear seems uncertain about his own direction of travel. After cutting the distance between us in half, however, my lot improves considerably. The bear has started toward us, the wind has at least remained constant, and a small fresh-water stream emerging from the bluff transects the beach, providing a six-foot-deep trench in which I can maneuver freely. Andrei and I have a last-minute conference in which neither of us can convey anything to the other except a sense of excitement. Then I work my way into the creek bed while Andrei takes up a position seventy yards behind me on the bluff.

The bear remains a relatively abstract presence at first as he closes leisurely to a range of one hundred yards. Then the mood changes. This is a real grizzly now, all fang and claw and shoulder hump as he hones in relentlessly upon my position. For an archer, a frontal shot on an advancing bear is pointless, so my tactical goal is to be twenty yards downwind when he crosses the creek and gives me a broadside. The problem is that the bear is tacking back and forth across the tide line. Every time I move laterally and peek over the top of the ditch, he is bearing straight down upon me. My stalk is starting to seem less a matter of getting within bow range than of surviving the process.

Forty yards and closing. It is time to start shutting systems down. Our brains come equipped with warning devices that tell us to retreat before we get within what I call pouncing range, the inner circle within which a bear is likely to swat first and ask questions later. If you are going to bowhunt bears, you have to learn to pull that fuse.

Thirty yards. I have crab-crawled down the creek bed again only to find the bear pointed right at me once more. Visions surface of Ray's eight-foot encounter the previous year. I try not to wonder just how many of those we can expect to survive without incident.

Twenty yards. As in the emergency landing of an airplane, the ground seems to be rushing closer and my options are narrowing fast. I finger the arrow on the bowstring and scoot toward the surf one last time, fully prepared for the fact that when I next see the bear I may be looking at his belly button as he comes over the bank on top of me. I make one simple promise: I will not lose it. I have come too far to do no better than that.

The bear does not appear on schedule. I ease my head above the bank. Finally, he has done what I needed him to do, which is to stop and root about in the tide line. He is twenty yards away, broadside. He is asking for my arrow.

It is time to shut down more systems. Matters of range and trajectory are not the way of the instinctive archer, and to consider such things now is to invent new ways to miss huge targets at close range. My right hand finds the corner of my mouth, savoring the familiar tensions of the longbow. The bear steps forward, opening up the final corner of his chest. The release is perfect, effortless and dreamy. Now, as they say, things really start to get interesting.

The arrow buries itself in the sweet spot behind the bear's shoulder and I know at once that I have killed him. His hindquarters sag at the impact. A chilling bellow rises above the surf's slap and the great ursine head swings toward the sound of the bowstring as I hit the dirt like a Marine receiving hostile fire on a beachhead. I know the bear has not seen me, and that if he charges the sound of the shot, his momentum will probably carry him right over my head, affording my arrow and Andrei's carbine precious seconds. There is a detached sense of timelessness as I press my face into the sand behind the creek bank, and it occurs to me that this may be what it feels like to recognize one's own death and accept it.

The sudden crack of Andrei's carbine punctuates the air. This cannot be good, but since I am already doing the one and only thing that I can do, I do nothing more. Just another day at the beach, I tell myself as I plaster myself into the sand and await the worst, but there are no more shots, and I know from past experience that the standard Soviet manner of dealing with real bear trouble is to empty the carbine's magazine as rapidly as possible. Finally I can stand it no longer and raise my head above the bank in time to see the bear stagger over the bluff at the top of the beach.

There is nothing in the air but the wild exhilaration of survival as Andrei and I regroup at the head of the creek. "He's dead!" I shout, confirming my confidence in the hit in every language I know, which unfortunately does not include Russian. *"Muerto! Finis!"* Andrei is dancing about like a leprechaun. Even after a lifetime here in the bush, he has never seen anything quite like this. I pantomime the arrow's entrance into the bear's chest with my forefinger against my own rib cage. "Shoot?" I ask, pointing to the carbine. "Ground?"

"Da," he assures me, adding his own pantomime by pointing the rifle's muzzle toward the sand. "Ground!"

Then everything is perfect. We walk slowly toward the spot where I last marked the bear. There is bright blood upon the gravel. Atop the bluff, the trail leads toward the *slanek*. Andrei is ready to go, but the trail is young and there is nothing but shadow ahead of us on the ground as the long northern twilight fades from the western sky. This is no good and I know it. There are no clouds and the trail will keep. I make the decision. We will return in the morning.

The bowman walks in front as he must under these circumstances, alone with his thoughts. This is the first time I have ever seen the sun rise from the Pacific, and I understand at once why the image is so compelling to the Japanese. The sea is quiet, the morning clear. Offshore, gulls are working the tideline. This could indeed be just another day at the beach.

I return to the creek bed, a piece of real estate whose details I now know my memory will carry for the rest of my life. I talk everyone through the scenario of the bear's approach and the shot. Now it is time to get down to business.

We pick up the blood trail where we left it the night before. As expected, it crosses eighty yards of open ground to the edge of the brush. Cautiously, I circle one way and Ray searches the other as the Russians stand with their carbines ready. Then I hear Ray shout and I know that the trail is over.

Beside the dead bear, there is relief and amazement to go around. The bear is so big, the bow so small. Only when we turn him and begin to skin do I sense discordance. "Looks like you hit him a bit back," Ray observes.

"I hit him right behind the shoulder," I reply.

But there it is, a red spot low in the paunch. We bend forward. I explore the strange wound with my finger. "Bullet," Andrei suddenly announces, and then it all becomes clear.

The postmortem examination is conducted by Drs. Barker, Stalmaster and Belyev. The findings are as follows:

The subject is a mature male grizzly bear, *Ursus arctos*, estimated weight: 250 kg, estimated age: seven years.

There are healed scars in the skin about the face and muzzle consistent with previous fighting. Otherwise, relevant findings are confined to the chest and abdomen. There is a linear incision in the skin over the right chest wall, 3 cm in greatest length. A foreign body is present inside the chest cavity, consisting of a wooden cylinder attached to a sharpened piece of steel, overall length 20 cm. The foreign body is consistent with an arrow and broadhead and is labeled as Exhibit A. The right lung is collapsed. The left lung is punctured. The pericardium is intact. There are an estimated two liters of blood in the chest cavity. There are circular wounds in the skin on both sides of the midline of the anterior abdominal wall. This wound is consistent with a projectile from a high-velocity, small-caliber rifle. The forensic pathology committee concludes that the cause of the subject's death is hemo-pneumothorax due to penetrating chest trauma. The wound to the anterior abdomen is incidentally noted.

"Forget it," Ray says pointing to the bullet hole. "It is a non-event. It didn't happen. Bury it right here on the beach."

I appreciate his concern for my feelings. But he doesn't know that the first five hundred words of this story have already been written, that promises have been made.

I am walking along the beach with the two Andreis. It is important to talk this through. Andrei Shepin explains. The bear was too close and mortally wounded. He felt that the situation was dangerous and that he had to turn the bear with his carbine. I explain in turn that while I respect his judgment, bowhunting is a different business in which the *object* is to get too close, and then to wound the bear mortally once you are there. We talk on as we walk down the beach with the bear hide, and that night in camp we drink a lot of vodka and talk some more. In the end, everyone seems to understand.

And there you have it: the truth, the whole truth. Some accomplishments in the sporting life are meant to have asterisks beside them and I suppose this is one of them. Hell, Roger Maris learned to live with his and I will learn to live with mine.

Bowhunters being the way they are, there will be those of the eager opinion that I did not leave Russia with a bow-killed grizzly. Of course, opinions are like certain parts of the human anatomy in that everybody gets to have one. The important thing is simply this: I know what happened on that lonely stretch of beach. So do Ray and Andrei. Now you do, too.

And what of the bear himself? Oh, yes; that was another promise, wasn't it? Well, I have kept that one too. Since the moment that I first saw him, I have not let one day pass without honoring his spirit. I doubt that I ever will.

TWELVE

Thank You, Sensei

They compose poems to their knives.

Frank Herbert, *Dune*

HERBERT'S MYTHICAL FREMEN were a wild, independent race whose men celebrated their weapons in song and whose women threw their children at their enemies in battle.

No, I have never written a poem to a knife. And for that matter, Sheli never tossed either of the kids at anyone, although I doubt she would have hesitated if the offending party had been stealing one of her horses.

In fact, I never thought much of people who get misty eyed about *things,* as opposed to other people, or Labrador retrievers. Not that I am completely incapable of becoming attached to inanimate objects. Actually, there is quite a collection of insentient tools and devices that I care for, ranging from the over and under that my father gave me as a graduation present twenty years ago to a bush plane that I once owned. But as important as all these things have been to me, I never became truly sentimental about any of them. I never gave them names. They are ultimately means that I employ to satisfy ends. They are, well, things.

Then there is the matter of my longbow. In fact, I own half a dozen functional longbows as well as a few relics, but when I refer to *my* longbow no one has any doubt about which bow I am speaking. It comes with numbers (66″, 70#) as all bows do, but these numbers seem irrelevant, the way that the numerical dimensions of a canvas might seem irrelevant to the discussion of a fine painting.

And while I have not gone quite so far as to write a poem to my bow, I have given it a name, something I have never done before for anything that cannot talk or fetch ducks. I would like to tell you now about my bow and the name that I have given it. I think that the process of my descent into this blithery state of romanticism may hold lessons for us all, including those who hunt with longbows and those who hunt with rifles, and perhaps even those who do not hunt at all.

This bow has been with me for ten years. My good friend and master bowyer Dick Robertson of Hamilton, Montana, was the midwife who coaxed the bow from the wood. I could now hold forth about the nature of that wood, the grain of the limbs, and the character of the riser, and I realize that my failure to do so may offend any traditional bowyers who happen to read this piece. It should bother them; those woods are the essence of their chosen craft. But I do not make my own bows, at least not yet, and so it would seem specious of me to discuss such matters as if I knew what I were talking about. Of course, I can appreciate an Osage stave coughed up by a weathered fence post. Anyone can. But, I don't care what kind of wood my bow is made of, not really. What I care about is what the bow does in my hands.

Learning to shoot a longbow is like learning to play a guitar, fly an airplane, or practice medicine. There is never a moment at which one can step back from the canvas, sign the corner, and say that the work is done. The skill acquisition curve is long and steep, and the initial phase can be frankly humiliating. In medieval England, boys were required to practice with the longbow daily on the village green, a civil defense exercise that eventually paid handsome dividends at the Battle of Crecy. For those of us who grew up with less archery in our childhood, it takes an odd combination of personality traits to learn the art well enough to hunt responsibly with stick and string: discipline, stubbornness, pride, and a deep sense of romantic commitment. There are certainly other, easier means to shoot things. The way of the longbow is not for everyone.

The last printed word on the subject comes not from any of the authors of bowhunting's modern revival, but from Eugen Herrigel, the once obscure German academic whose experiences in Japan gave birth to *Zen in the Art of Archery*. This slender volume has enjoyed a cult following of sorts for decades. It is interesting to note that most of the book's campus devotees have never held a bow in their hands, while most archers I know have never heard of Eugen Herrigel, who after all never really shot much of anything. Suffice it to say that Herrigel's minor masterpiece should be required reading for anyone who really wants to learn about shooting a bow, or for that matter, about doing anything else.

Able as he is, even Herrigel founders on the rock of trying to explain the unexplainable, which is why I've always been happy to leave the book's coffeehouse metaphysics alone. Its enduring and entirely transcultural theme concerns the relationship between discipline and realization. At one point, for example, Herrigel admits that his instructor required him to practice his form for *four years* before permitting him to shoot an arrow at a target. On another occasion, Herrigel becomes mistakenly convinced that he has learned the secret of the proper release in a moment of enlightenment. When he demonstrates this erroneous discovery to his archery master, the old man shrugs and informs his student that he will never be able to speak to him again.

I do not pretend that these anecdotes have revealed to me the Nature of the Universe. I do suggest that they are worth keeping in mind when the bowman is spewing arrows about the practice range in confusion.

As a visible proponent of traditional archery, I am often called upon to explain the technical, as well as philosophical, differences between shooting the longbow and the vastly more popular compound. Since the folks asking these questions are often more familiar with firearms than they are with bows and arrows, I have come up with a simple analogy which is not intended to offend anyone, although occasionally it does. Shooting a compound bow is like shooting a rifle and shooting a longbow is like shooting a shotgun. It's really that simple.

While shooting a rifle properly obviously involves its own measure of technique, getting a bullet from point A to point B also involves a heavy measure of ballistics, which is why so much writing on the subject is devoted to technical details. Wingshooting, on the other hand, is generally conceded to involve more art than science, which is why the shotgun literature is full of fuzzy metaphors rather than charts and tables. If you understand this distinction and can appreciate the difference between aiming and pointing, you can appreciate the difference between shooting a compound bow with sights and the traditional style of archery called instinctive, for want of a better term.

As is the case with high house station 8's on the skeet range, these are difficult things to teach and difficult things to learn. Some people, of course, are born with the ability to point where they are looking, while others may never get the hang of it no matter how hard they practice or how much instruction they receive. But anyone who picks up a longbow for the first time and pulls one hand back to convert the bow's potential energy into arrow flight that is straight, honest, and true has much to learn. And it is the bow, I finally decided, that is the teacher.

Longbows, you see, do not make mistakes. There are no cables or pulleys or sights to stand in the way between the bowman and the bow. Except for the occasional twist of the bowstring, there is no tuning to distract attention from the task at hand or provide excuses when arrows wind up in places we did not ask them to visit. One may say "The bowstring hit my arm guard" when an arrow dives pathetically into the ground, but this is not an accurate statement. What one really means to say, of course, is: "I hit my arm guard with the bowstring." There is a difference.

After more years of formal education than I care to count, I have certainly had my share of good teachers. One of the best was a diminutive Japanese violinist who also happened to hold a seventh degree black belt in *aikido*. I studied this most sublime martial arts discipline with him for several years before I moved on to places where there were more moose than *aikido* instructors, and my geographic inability to continue this training has been one of the few disappointments in my life.

I can see great parallels between the disciplines of *aikido* and archery. The energy I put into each endeavor was reflected back at me precisely and honestly. In each undertaking, attempts to over-control lead immediately to failure. The rise of temper is inevitably rebuffed by the art itself. And both undertakings required a master, a *sensei*.

As I came to terms with my longbow, it finally became clear to me: every arrow that I shot had a lesson to teach. I just needed to be alert enough to figure out what each lesson was.

I do not know how many animals I have harvested with my longbow. I do know that the list covers the waterfront from grouse to grizzly and includes nine or ten species of big game animals in between.

I certainly remember the first, the caribou bull described in this collection's first chapter. To this day, I have no recollection of drawing the bowstring. The shot just happened, and I might as well have been a bystander to the process. In the shot's aftermath, I first realized that I was onto something special.

One of those I remember most clearly was the black bear on the beach in southeastern Alaska, the one who was at least willing to pretend that he wanted to kill me. I cannot blame the bear, since I initiated the encounter. The hunter became the hunted, however, and since I was not carrying a firearm, there was finally nothing to do but ask my longbow to drive an arrow through the middle of the bear, and it did just that. The bear's hide is on my wall now. So is the arrow. I could hunt with it again if I wanted to, but I don't. One favor like that is enough to ask.

I always told myself that I would retire my longbow if and when I shot a grizzly with it. Years of hunting at a maniac pace in hard terrain and difficult climatic conditions had taken their toll. I have used the bow to whack bushes calling moose and as an ice ax to self-arrest while glissading down snowfields on goat hunts. Its limbs have tasted rock and sleet and blood. I imagined retiring the bow the way one retires a bird dog after years of loyal service. The dog lives out the rest of its time in front of the fireplace; the bow could recline in the moose antlers above the fireplace.

But then this spring the grizzly was suddenly there in front of me, just as I had always known he would be someday. I asked my longbow to put the arrow behind his shoulder, and the bow did just that. And when I finally knelt beside the dead bear to marvel at what the bow and I had done together, I had to ask myself about putting out to pasture an instrument as marvelous as this. Could I really do such a thing? No.

It was, however, time for a face-lift. Well aware of my bow's history and the role it had played in my life, Dick Robertson accepted it gracefully back into his shop. He told me later that he tried to imagine the story behind each of the nicks and dings as he sanded them out. Dick is just that kind of guy.

With the finish gone and the limbs and riser back down to bare wood, I realized that this was the time to rescue my bow from anonymity and give it a name. It had certainly earned the honor. I thought about the lessons each of the zillion arrows I had shot from it held for me. I remembered *aikido* class protocol, when the thing to do after having the instructor send you fifteen feet through the air to land on the hard mat was to roll immediately to your feet, bow, and express gratitude for the insight this maneuver afforded.

It was time to say it again. Thank you, *sensei*.

Bear Country

> . . . *(The grizzly) is said more frequently to attack a man*
> *on meeting with him than to flee from him. When the*
> *Indians are about to go in quest of the white bear, previous to*
> *their departure they paint themselves and perform all those*
> *superstitious rites commonly observed when*
> *they are about to make war on a neighboring nation.*
>
> Meriwether Lewis, April 13, 1805

THOSE VENTURING INTO the American wilderness have always had an uneasy relationship with bears, especially in Alaska where bear stories are always near the epicenter of regional myth. Even today, few problems in bush medicine arouse as much apprehension as bear attacks, although they are among the most uncommon disasters the outdoorsman is likely to encounter, even in the heart of bear country. Of all the various sorts of outdoor recreationists likely to run into bears in the wild, however, bowhunters face some special problems. Answering the call of sheep, caribou, or moose usually involves spending time in serious grizzly country. Making noise, a time-honored and perfectly reasonable means of keeping casual hikers from surprising bears at close range, just doesn't fit into the bowhunter's agenda. And in contrast to riflemen, our basic hunting tools are all but useless in defense against dangerous game. In bear country, no one needs to know more about the prevention and management of bear attacks than bowhunters.

The importance of preventing injury as opposed to treating it is a recurrent theme in wilderness medicine, with good reason. Being called upon to render first aid to the victim of a serious mauling in the back country can challenge anyone's medical skills. Most bear attacks are preventable, and anyone who plans to bowhunt the Far North needs to know how to do just that.

Because bear attacks are such rare events, there is surprisingly little scientific information about their causes. Anyone who has spent much time in bear country seems to have a story to tell, but organizing this body of anecdotal information in a way that allows accurate analysis is a difficult task. Perhaps the best effort can be found in Steven Herrero's book, *Bear Attacks: Their Cause and Avoidance* (Winchester Press, 1985). If this study has a flaw from the bowhunter's perspective, it is that a disproportionate amount of its information is based on encounters between people and bears in national parks. Habituated park bears certainly cause more than their share of problems, but they are entirely different animals than their wild counterparts. Nonetheless, Herrero's book is generally authoritative and should be mandatory reading for any bowhunter visiting Alaska for the first time.

I have been fortunate enough to spend a fair share of time in bear country, and the presence of these remarkable animals has consistently enriched my enjoyment of the outdoor experience. My personal definition of an aggressive bear is one that recognizes me as a human being and does anything other than run away. According to these terms, my own score card of encounters with aggressive bears is fairly brief, and consists for the most part, in addition to several incidents described earlier, of threat displays by black bear sows with cubs and curious approaches by young male grizzlies. The many other occasions on which I found myself close enough to a bear in the wild for the animal to be aware of my presence all ended with a rapid retreat on the part of the bear.

On the other hand, I remember one morning spent fighting my way through the willows along the bank of a remote Alaska river while hiking into sheep country. I finally climbed up on a rock outcropping to glass for game. From there I could see a blonde grizzly sow and two cubs working their way through the brush on the opposite side of the river. It was a beautiful sight and the bears never knew I was there, but I realized that if either the sow or I had chosen the other side of the river to walk along that morning, a close-range encounter in the brush would have been inevitable. I was alone and unarmed except for a longbow. The nearest medical care other than my own was hundreds of miles away. If such experiences don't make you think, you probably don't belong in bear country in the first place.

URSUS ARCTOS HORRIBILIS

The disappearance of the grizzly from much of its historic range is one of the great tragedies of the American experience. The good news is that much of Alaska and western Canada now support as many of the big bears as they ever did, a fact that sound management and habitat protection will hopefully ensure for future generations of men and bears alike. On the far side of the former Asian land bridge where the grizzly originated, the Soviet Far East still supports tremendous numbers of bears biologically identical to our own. While grizzly encounters outside national parks are rare events in the lower forty-eight states, any bowhunter planning a trip to one of these areas needs to develop some bear smarts in order to have a safe and enjoyable stay in the bush.

My own thinking about grizzly encounters can be summarized easily. While the big bears are always *potentially* dangerous, they are *predictably* dangerous only in a few well-defined situations: when a bear is wounded or habituated to human presence; when a bear is surprised at close range or behaving defensively toward an established food source; or when the bear in question is a sow accompanied by cubs. Treating grizzlies with respect at all times and taking great care in these specific situations has allowed me to share the woods harmoniously with them, at least so far.

Again, the difference between grizzlies in the wild and those in national parks cannot be overemphasized. Several years ago, a hiker in Glacier National Park was charged spontaneously by a bear falling into none of the previously mentioned dangerous categories. The ranger investigating the mauling reported to the press that this unprovoked attack represented "normal grizzly bear behavior." Fortunately, this statement is totally untrue. If it were accurate, no one in Alaska would be able to set foot outside, and I would be long dead. What the ranger should have said is that this attack represented normal behavior for a bear in a national park, which explains why the handful of bears left in Yellowstone and Glacier bother me a whole lot more than all the wild ones I have dealt with elsewhere.

Avoiding grizzly mishaps is a lot like bowhunting in one respect: it helps to be aware of the bears before they are aware of you. Bowhunters have an advantage over most casual hikers in that we are used to being intuitively alert to the wind and the presence of game. Unless you are in thick cover or being downright careless, you should have time to practice some preventive medicine whenever you run into a bear in the wild.

The first thing to do whenever you spot a grizzly during the course of a hunt is to stop whatever you are doing and watch the bear. In the first place, grizzlies are always worth watching, no matter how many of them you have seen before. Furthermore, a quiet period of study will allow you to make some important observations. Is the bear a sow with cubs? Is it guarding a dead moose or similar food source? What is the animal's most likely route of travel? Don't continue stalking, glassing, or hiking until you have analyzed the bear situation completely.

Suppose circumstances have put you closer to the grizzly than you want to be. Bowhunters are used to being close to wild animals, but anything under a hundred yeads is too close to a grizzly unless you have a good reason to be there. Remember that a bear can cover that distance in a matter of seconds if motivated to do so. If the bear is unaware of your presence, I would begin a cautious, quiet retreat, paying attention to the bear and the wind: a stalk in reverse, if you will. The safest bear encounter is always one in which the bear never knows you were there. I would also, however, make a mental note of the location of the nearest climbing tree.

While grizzlies don't really climb trees the way black bears do, they have certain capabilities that need to be kept in mind. They can haul themselves quite a way up a tree with stout branches, they can reach an awfully long way above the ground, and they can simply bulldoze over most of the scrubby trees in Alaska if they really want to. To be safe, you need to be at least fifteen feet off the ground in a fairly substantial tree. If one meeting those requirements isn't available, it's time to pursue other options.

Let's assume that our hypothetical bear has now given you some indication that he is aware of your presence. Perhaps he has stood up for a better look (this common behavior is *not* the beginning of a charge, by the way) or given you a *whoof!* or similar curiosity vocalization. The hair on the back of your own neck has probably started to rise a bit, as well it should. What you do next may well determine the outcome of the encounter.

The bear now knows that you are something. It is time to let him know what, since wild grizzlies are almost always as anxious to avoid people as you are to avoid them. No more sneaking around in typical bowhunter fashion! Let the bear hear your voice. Give him your wind. Move deliberately, but let him have a good look.

Once the bear has identified you as the intrusive, foul-smelling *Homo sapiens* that you are, the encounter will probably end at once, as anyone who has spent time stalking bears well knows. But what if it doesn't? Some recommend dropping closer to the ground to reduce the threat attitude toward the bear. I worry that this tactic might produce further advance, because of curiosity or predatory instinct. I would remain upright, giving the bear a good look at me, and continue a slow, deliberate retreat. Don't gesture aggressively: grizzlies, in contrast to black bears, just don't bluff. And certainly don't run unless you are seconds away from a secure place to run to—a bearproof cabin, a vehicle, or an adequate climbing tree. Running can clearly evoke an aggressive response from a grizzly. Keep the animal in sight if at all possible so that you can gauge its response to whatever you are doing.

Continuing down the path of the worst-case scenario, let us assume that our grizzly has clearly recognized you as a human being, but instead of disappearing into the brush according to the script, he is now advancing in your direction. What you do next should depend in part on your observations of the bear. Understanding ursine body language is important. If the animal appears to be a curious young male, as is often the case, I would step up my shouting and add some arm-waving body language of my own. On the other hand, if the bear is demonstrating serious threat behavior such as jaw popping or neck posturing, a quiet retreat is more appropriate. Avoid direct eye contact, an insult in bear language. Finally, if the bear is a sow with cubs, it is time to recognize that you have a problem. If a tree is available, start climbing. If you have an adequate firearm, be ready to use it.

One common recommendation is to drop something, such as an article of clothing, in your path as you retreat, the theory being that this will allow the bear to confirm your human identity by smell. While this maneuver might buy a little time in some situations, it isn't going to accomplish much if the bear is an angry sow. One item I would not discard is a frame backpack, unless it is full of moose meat. There are several well-documented instances of mauling victims avoiding serious injury because the bear spent more time chewing on the backpack than on the person wearing it.

All right, partner: it's white-knuckle time. Despite all this good advice and politically correct behavior on your part, the bear is now obviously charging. The nearest climbing tree is a hundred miles away on the other side of the Brooks Range. Your only weapon is the suddenly diminutive bow in your hand. How did a nice guy like you get in a jam like this? Better ask how you're going to get out!

First—don't panic. This is admittedly a far easier recommendation to make from behind a word processor than it is in the field, especially when the field is filling up with angry bear. Nonetheless, it is impossible to outrun a grizzly, and analysis of grizzly attacks clearly indicates that running may make matters worse.

Second—protect your vital parts. The head, neck, and abdomen are the areas most vulnerable to serious injury. Assume the "cannonball" position with hands clasped behind your neck, chin tucked down onto your chest, and knees drawn up against your belly. If you are wearing a backpack, keep it between you and the bear if at all possible.

Third—play dead. Active resistance doesn't accomplish much *if the attacking bear is a grizzly.* It is important to realize that the vast majority of grizzly maulings do not result in death or critical injury. Again, analysis of previous attacks suggests that waiting things out passively is the best survival tactic.

So much for the exceptional situation in which a *potentially* dangerous bear becomes an *actually* dangerous bear. What about the far more important issue of avoiding an attack from a bear that you knew (or should have known) was likely to cause trouble?

There isn't much to be done about sows with cubs other than to avoid them. If you happen to stumble into a clump of alders containing this particular combination of bears, you probably aren't going to enjoy the rest of the afternoon very much. The usual bear country advice for avoiding this sort of chance encounter—traveling in large groups, making lots of noise, and staying out of the heavy cover—doesn't apply very well to the typical bowhunter. Nonetheless, if I have to travel along a salmon stream or similar area of high bear density, I'm not above putting my hunting priorities on hold and making some noise, especially if I am alone.

Bears acting aggressively toward food sources are another matter. Such potential trouble spots are easily identified and all too often of our own making. Short of blundering into a grizzly guarding a dead moose, there isn't much excuse for most encounters of this kind.

The most prevalent form of bear bait in the typical wilderness setting is your own camp. Remember what efficient scavengers bears are. There should be no such thing as leftovers in bear country. Eat it and burn whatever is left. Wash all dishes and utensils completely, in free running water some distance downstream from camp if possible. If you have been fortunate enough to harvest game, store the meat at a safe distance from camp, preferably in an open area you can study from a distance for signs of unwelcome visitors. If you have just butchered a moose or caribou, clean up carefully before you enter your tent again, and store the soiled clothing safely with the meat. Have a firearm available in camp if feasible, and above all never store food or anything that smells like food in a tent you plan to sleep in. This all sounds like extra work and it is. I'll certainly admit to breaking some of these rules from time to time, but I've heard enough "bear in camp" stories to know that it is foolish to do so.

THE UNDERRATED BLACK BEAR

I'm the first to admit that black bears don't arouse the visceral respect inside me that their larger cousins command. Anyone who has blown as many stalks on these animals as I have may have to remind themself that black bears are capable of aggressive behavior. Certainly, anyone who has watched a large black bear tear a log apart while feeding knows that they have the physical capacity to cause bodily harm. While the most dangerous black bears are always those that have become habituated to human presence, there are enough well-documented instances of serious attacks by their wild counterparts to justify respect for the species under any circumstances.

Why does the wary, secretive black bear occasionally become aggressive? The most common reasons are the same ones noted earlier with respect to the grizzly: habituation, surprise at close quarters, defense of food sources, and cubs. There are two other situations in which black bears occasionally become troublemakers.

The first, quite obviously, stems from the fact that black bears are a popular quarry for bowhunters. Any wounded bear is a potentially dangerous bear. Setting off on a blood trail alone and unarmed is ill-advised, no matter what kind of bear is involved.

Secondly, analysis of those rare situations in which a black bear has initiated an unprovoked attack on a human suggests that the bear's motives are often predatory. For some reason, simple hunger can occasionally motivate the opportunistic black bear to treat people as prey. Such transgressions really shouldn't be surprising, since the black bear's basic approach to the world around him is to treat it as one vast, varied food source.

Since the black bear is by nature much less aggressive than the grizzly, there is an important difference in the response to belligerent behavior by each species. If the offender is a black bear, don't play dead. Fight back! Documented instances of a victim warding off a serious grizzly attack by active resistance are rare. This is not the case with black bears, who may just be looking for an easy meal. At every step with a black bear who does anything other than run away when I want him to, I would be more aggressive than I would be in similar circumstances with a grizzly. The black bear is just as capable of inflicting harm, but his personality makes aggressiveness a more effective approach to deterrence.

SELF-DEFENSE IN BEAR COUNTRY

While I have not personally hunted with a rifle for many years, firearms do have a place in bear country, even in a bowhunting camp.

The best form of self-defense, of course, is understanding bear habits and behavior so that you can stay out of confrontational situations in the first place. Unfortunately, this isn't always possible. Approaching a downed animal in the field after an overnight wait is always risky in bear country, as is the long pack trip out with the meat. At times like this, I prefer to have some company and a rifle along. I also like to have a firearm available in camp no matter how clean and tidy it's kept. Remember that the difference between your trophy caribou and bear bait is largely a matter of arbitrary perspective.

What kind of firearm is appropriate under such circumstances? Pistols enjoy a traditional popularity among bowhunters because of their obvious convenience. However, pistols are marginal at best for back-up on black bear hunts, and even the larger calibers lack the punch to stop motivated grizzlies. Until quite recently, there were *no* documented instances in the state of Alaska of someone successfully defending himself against an attacking grizzly with a handgun. Short-barreled, 12-gauge shotguns have their advocates, but penetration tests conducted by the Alaska Department of Fish and Game in a study specifically designed to determine the optimal firearms for bear protection did not give satisfactory marks to any shotgun. My own feeling is that one should either carry a definitive bear stopper (a .338 caliber rifle or larger) or consider yourself unarmed and act accordingly. While I like to have a rifle along in the sort of high risk situation described earlier, in the field I usually just carry my longbow and remember that the bears are tougher than I am. So far, so good.

Another option that may be of value to bowhunters in certain situations is a newly developed product called Counter Assault®, a highly irritating mixture of pepper derivatives packed into an aerosol can that can be worn conveniently on the belt. While I have had no direct experience with this product, expert opinion suggests that it may be quite effective in deterring aggressive bears. Because of its convenience, this might be an appropriate means of defense in situations in which the hunter would otherwise be unarmed.

MEDICAL AND LEGAL ISSUES IN BEAR COUNTRY

With the exception of a few cases of severe jitters, I have never had to treat the victim of an unwanted bear encounter. I have had lots of opportunity to talk to other physicians who have done so, however, and it seems to be a universally unsettling experience. Among other things, serious bear maulings often involve major facial injuries, which in addition to posing a threat to the victim's airway and life can have a strong psychological impact on the rescuer.

Here are a few simple guidelines for the nonprofessional called upon to render emergency aid in the field. Again, don't panic. No matter how bad things look, most victims survive bear maulings, even the more serious ones. Make a quick, accurate assessment of the situation and take the first steps in the field management of any trauma victim: ensure that the airway is patent, determine that respirations are adequate, stop external bleeding by direct pressure, and stabilize the spine if appropriate. A complete review of how to accomplish these goals is beyond the scope of this discussion. If you are unfamiliar with these techniques, you should acquire some basic skills before heading into the bush whether there are bears there or not.

Be alert to the possibility that a dangerous animal may still be at large and take whatever steps are necessary to prevent another attack. Remember that turning a rescuer into a victim is a major step backwards in all wilderness medicine situations, especially if it is happening to you. Wounds inflicted by animals' fangs and claws are notoriously dirty and susceptible to infection. Once the critical care aspects of the medical situation have been stabilized, wash wounds with soap and water. Empiric administration of antibiotics is generally appropriate if they are available. Remember that your tetanus immunization status should be current— *before* you set off into the wilderness in the first place.

Once the injured party has been evacuated to a source of definitive medical care, analyze what happened and why. Don't forget to notify the game warden or other appropriate authority, especially if you or someone in your party has fired at the bear in self-defense. Your actions may have significant legal implications. While Alaska law allows reasonable action in the defense of life or property, it is mandatory to report all such encounters as soon as practical if this statute is invoked. If there is evidence to suggest that the offending bear is still a threat to others, the game warden (known as the Fish and Wildlife Protection officer in Alaska) may have to take appropriate action against the animal, but that is his decision, not yours, under all but emergency circumstances.

THEIR WORLD AND OURS

The focus of this chapter has forced us to look at bears in their most threatening context. They can always be dangerous to humans, although most of the time they aren't. Despite misconceptions, bears are always capable of being hazardous, and not always because the human victim was doing something malicious or foolish.

And yet it would be irresponsible to close without emphasizing how unlikely any of this is to happen, even to those of us fortunate enough to spend time in bear country. Bears are marvelous and fascinating animals, not the least because of their power, courage, and their everpresent potential for danger. We ourselves are a haughty species in our own right. It does us good to be reminded from time to time that we are not the only tough guys afoot in the woods. Anyone who has watched a grizzly tear up an acre of tundra digging for rodents or run into a black bear family only to be backed right down by a jaw-popping sow should realize how much richer the outdoor world is because of the bears' presence in it. Bears speak to something primal in the recesses of the human brain, the same quarter of our instinct that makes us hunt in the first place. We should all be thankful for that.

Bears don't need artificial inflation of their stature. They project enough stature on their own. What bears do need is basic understanding of their character and habits so that we can share the woods with them without becoming the subjects of campfire legend ourselves.

Tundra Journal

AUGUST 22. As I watched the Beaver back-taxi to the downwind edge of the little lake, I readied myself mentally. There it was: the roar of all that horsepower as the pilot advanced the throttle, the receding drone of the engine as the floatplane disappeared over the horizon, and then the silence. The contrast between the busy noise of all that technology and the utter quiet that follows its departure always leaves me awed. As I scanned the rolling tundra around the lake, I felt a familiar flush of excitement flavored by agoraphobia and the certain knowledge that the country was far larger than me.

Along with pilot Greg Bell and hunting partners Dick LeBlond and Joe Kelly, I had spent the afternoon flying the Mulchatna River drainage west of the Alaska range. I was looking for concentrations of caribou in the kind of country I favor for bowhunting them: dry enough to allow good hiking, open enough to glass and cover some ground, but with enough breaks in the terrain to allow opportunities to stalk to the intimate range our chosen equipment demands. Even in country this size, finding just the right location for base camp can take some time, but the rolling tundra surrounding the lake we finally settled on seemed to fill these requirements to perfection.

Since we could not legally hunt big game that day after being airborne, we spent the rest of the afternoon securing the camp against the inevitable arrival of foul weather. Once our chores were finished, we set off across country to scout and hunt ptarmigan. The white birds were there all right, but they were hopelessly wild. While I found myself longing briefly for my dog and my double, we had nothing in camp but longbows, and there were no ptarmigan in the skillet later when we settled in for our first night on the tundra.

AUGUST 23: We awoke to the steady rhythm of rain falling against the tent fly. I burrowed deeper into my sleeping bag and dozed for another hour, hoping the weather would break—to no avail. By the time the dull gray glow in the east matured into daylight, it was apparent that we would be hunting in rain gear.

After glassing for an hour from the ridge behind our camp, Joe headed south toward a series of low hills where several bands of caribou were grazing. Dick and I set off to the north, into a broad valley dotted with potholes and scattered lines of brush. We spent the day battling the weather and looking at caribou—lots of caribou. Since both of us had been fortunate enough to take good bulls with our bows before, neither of us felt like stalking the first animals we saw.

By late afternoon, we were damp and pleasantly tired after a long day of hiking. Just as we were about to turn back toward camp, Dick caught a glimpse of a velvet antler tine sticking up out of a distant line of willows. My spotting scope revealed a group of five bulls, three of which were of trophy quality. After confirming a few landmarks, we set off at double time to try to intercept them.

As we worked our way through the maze of creeks and beaver dams on the valley floor, the drizzle we had been hunting in all day became a downpour. When we located the caribou again, they were feeding their way into the wind on a bench between two willow-choked creek beds. The terrain was ideal for stalking, since the creek banks offered good cover and we could keep track of the caribou as they moved by watching their antlers above the brush. Dick was elected to make the first stalk while I circled around downwind to await developments.

After completing my own end-around play, I peeked over the edge of the creek bank to find an excellent bull grazing head down some forty-five yards away. While this would have been a shot opportunity for some bowhunters, the range exceeded by a good fifteen yards the limitations I have disciplined myself to accept in my own shot selection. The wind and the cover were both favorable, and I thought there was an excellent opportunity to close to the range I needed. Caution paid off, however, as I noticed another, smaller caribou bedded down at the edge of the brush, facing me directly. There was nothing to do but hunker down and hope the big bull fed my way.

He didn't. After grazing his way randomly around the bench just beyond bow range, he finally moved off into the wind with his younger companion in tow. I spent the next hour paralleling their course without ever managing to close to the range I needed for a killing shot. Finally, the wind began to quarter across the bench. Having learned great respect for caribou noses over the years, I decided to retreat and hope things were going better for Dick, wherever he might be.

By the time I slogged my way back to camp, I was seriously wet. Not even hip waders and high-quality rain gear can keep a hunter dry after a day-long immersion in soaking underbrush, which is why I have such a high regard for quality woolens when hunting in Alaska. Once in camp, Joe and I spent an hour under our tarp trying to dry out without any sign of Dick. "Either this is real good," I noted, as the long northern twilight faded into darkness, "or it's real bad." Dick is a competent and experienced outdoorsman, but the long list of hazards out there could get the best of anyone.

We were midway through a desultory meal of canned something or another when Dick finally emerged from the gloom. One look at the grin on his face and the longbow held triumphantly overhead told us that he was late for the best of reasons.

After a round of relieved congratulations, Dick shared his story. Enjoying a favorable crosswind, he had been able to stay with the caribou until they bedded. Using the creek bottom for cover, he finally managed to stalk within twelve feet of one of the larger bulls. After a long, tense wait at point-blank range, one of the smaller bulls finally sensed his presence and stood up. When the rest of the caribou followed his lead, Dick anchored his quarry with a perfect double lung shot.

We all slept comfortably that night despite the drizzle outside the tent and the promise of a hard day of work to follow. The hunt was off to a tremendous start, and caribou backstraps were on the menu at last.

AUGUST 24. I like to think that packing meat is good for the soul. Somehow.

In Alaska, one seldom has the opportunity to retrieve downed game with a mechanized vehicle. This means that the excitement of big game hunting must be tempered by the understanding that well-placed arrows mean hard work, sometimes a lot of it. State law, not to mention a basic sense of outdoor ethics, demands the salvage of all usable meat. This requirement keeps the responsible hunter conscious of what he shoots and where he shoots it.

As I labored through a tangle of brush under the burden of a full pack, I reminded myself of all this. It seemed to help a little. There was half a caribou in my backpack, since Dick and I had excused Joe from packing chores so that he could go hunting.

Largely at my urging, Joe had taken up the bow some three seasons earlier. It is sometimes hard to convey to the uninitiated just how difficult bowhunting can be. Joe was understandably frustrated by the fact that he had yet to take his first big game animal with archery tackle. Accepting some responsibility for this state of affairs, I had encouraged Joe over breakfast to stop worrying about antlers and shoot the first mature caribou he could. Any such animal, taken fairly and cleanly, is a legitimate accomplishment for a bowhunter, especially when it is his first.

By the time Dick and I arrived back in camp with the meat, I was feeling very much like a guy who had just turned forty, which in fact I had. Rain was falling once more. Under somber skies, we constructed a meat storage rack a safe distance from camp in an open area we could observe for signs of raiding bears. Then we retreated back beneath the tarp to wait out the worst of the weather. Low clouds shrouded the hills rising around the little lake, and I began to wonder if we would ever see the sun again from this camp.

AUGUST 25. Arctic lichen is remarkable stuff. Clinging for its existence to some of the world's least hospitable soil, it is a source of beauty and nurture in an otherwise unbearably harsh land. No lichen, no herbivores; no herbivores, no carnivores. Here on the tundra, the food chain is that simple.

The ground cover on these treeless plains is highly complex. In addition to the yellow lichens favored by caribou, the tundra's carpet is woven from a varied array of mosses and low-lying plants whose interspecies relationships I do not pretend to understand. I do know that when the sun manages to burn its way through the low layers of stratus clouds that so often obscure this remote wilderness, as it finally did this morning, a rich array of color can appear suddenly where all was drab before. On days like this, I sometimes spend as much time looking at the ground underfoot as I do looking for caribou.

Alaska had finally served us up a glorious day. A dozen species of mushrooms sprouted within a bow's length of my perch on the hillside: amanitas, boletus, russulas, gypsies. Berries were everywhere. Today, it was my turn to be excused from packing detail for the simple reason that I now possessed the only valid caribou tag in camp. The previous evening, Joe had finally found himself in the right place at the right time and had taken his first animal with the bow.

By the time I finished my fresh blueberry lunch, I had looked over at least a hundred caribou without seeing one that I wanted. In common with almost all of Alaska's major caribou populations, the Mulchatna herd has fared well lately, and the area has been particularly good to my hunting partners and me over the years. There are many theories about this herd's movement patterns, but if I have learned anything about caribou it is that their only predictable character trait is unpredictability. I generally ignore the migrations anyway, since many eyes and noses make it difficult to approach within bow range. I prefer to concentrate on solitary bulls in the higher country prior to the rut. Now we seemed to be in the path of a lot of migrating cows and immature bulls, but I knew that some of the big boys had to be out there somewhere.

Suddenly, my meditation on the ecology of the barren ground caribou was interrupted as I swept my binoculars along a distant ridge. I noticed a brush pile silhouetted against the empty skyline in a place where there should have been no brush. As I watched, the brush pile rocked slowly from side to side. Then I switched from field glasses to spotting scope and obtained one definitive look at a world-class bull before he moved on across the horizon.

The bull was a long way off and there was no guarantee I would ever see him again, but he was the best caribou I had seen in some time. The decision was easy. A little over an hour later, I reached the ridgeline and sat down to glass the broad basin into which he had disappeared. After several minutes of searching, I saw the caribou again, grazing downhill half a mile below me in the company of a second, smaller bull. As usual, they were quartering into the wind.

When caribou are in their trot-and-graze mode of travel, they are deceptively difficult to overtake. The large bull was the kind of animal worth pulling out all stops for, however. After a long sprint down the mountain that I hoped would put me just in front of the caribou without letting them wind me, I eased around a patch of alders to find them grazing just beyond bow range. There was nothing to do but tighten the straps on my hip waders and set off on another circular approach around their route of travel.

My second attempt to set up an ambush ended much as the first had, as did several more. The wind simply made it impossible to get in front of them. Exhausted at last, I sat down to assess the situation. The stalk had started on the ridgeline four miles from camp. My efforts to intercept the bull had taken me two more miles down the back side of the hill toward the distant river. I will accept the responsibility of packing game any reasonable distance in order to take an exceptional animal with the bow, and so will the people with whom I hunt. Still, I knew that somewhere in that basin I had crossed the line between what is reasonable and what is not. It was time to do all of us one big favor and turn back.

I rose slowly from my hiding place and tipped my felt hat to the two bulls as they fed their way over the next little rise. I hope the old boy is still out there on the tundra somewhere, and that he still looks as magnificent as he did to me the afternoon he almost coaxed me beyond the limits of what I could do.

AUGUST 26. While no one likes to return from a hunt empty-handed, when one accepts the limitations imposed by traditional archery equipment, one also accepts the fact that many hunts will end without having the skinning knife leave its sheath. As the three of us sat glassing the tundra from the vantage point behind camp on the evening before our scheduled departure for civilization, I consoled myself with the knowledge that the hunt had allowed me to renew important friendships and enjoy one of my favorite wild places. These facts alone had made the rain and the hard miles worthwhile. Then Dick spotted the caribou.

"They went into a brush patch beside that lake," he said, pointing to a pothole a mile away to the north. "I just caught a glimpse of them, but there was at least one good bull."

I studied the area intently, but the caribou had disappeared. With two hours of hunting left, I didn't have a lot of options. "I'll take your word for it," I said, as I reached for my longbow and started down the hill.

Twenty minutes later, after a brisk but cautious approach, I eased over the little knoll to glass the area. With the perverse logic of their species, they had reversed directions completely. In fact, they were now almost to the base of our glassing hill where Dick and Joe still sat. While I didn't have a lot of time to study horns, I noted that there were three mature bulls in the band, one of which was exceptional.

I really don't enjoy running in hip waders, but I realized that I would have to once again if I were to have any chance of intercepting the caribou before dark. Thankful for the discipline of my regular summer running program, I dropped back over the skyline and took off. Fortunately, favorable terrain gave me all the cover I needed as I retraced my steps on the run.

The caribou arrived at the base of the hill just as I did. The next move was up to them. If they bore to the west, they would pass beyond the hill and my position would be hopeless. If they turned the other way, however, they would have to cross a narrow isthmus between two lakes with the wind, for once, at their backs. I decided to set up an ambush and hope they did what I needed them to do.

A dense patch of alders on the neck of land between the two lakes provided excellent cover, but it also prevented me from keeping the herd in sight. A caribou trail led down either side of the brush patch. If I set up in the middle of the alders, I would have a long shot no matter which trail they came down. I decided to gamble again and place myself near the corner of the brush patch. If the caribou came down the nearest trail, I would have an excellent shot; if they did anything else I would have no shot at all. And so in the final moment, a week of hard hunting came down to an intuitive guess as to the intentions of a dozen caribou, the most unpredictable big game animals in the north.

As I settled into the edge of the cover and nocked an arrow, the feather wind indicator on my bow string indicated that my scent would hit the trail about forty yards beyond my position. I marked the spot carefully. Even if everything went according to plan, the hunt would be over when the lead caribou reached that point on the trail.

Suddenly the clicking of caribou tendons just beyond the screen of alders announced the arrival of my quarry. The first caribou, a cow, appeared ten paces away, confirming that I had made all the right guesses. Then things began to happen too fast. The flow of events was beyond any pretense of control. A second cow filed past, then an immature bull, and suddenly the little strip of land was a milling sea of gray flanks and antlers. The largest of the mature bulls had not appeared yet. The lead cow was only a few steps away from the point at which she would wind me. A shootable bull was quartering by thirty yards away across the open ground. I realized that I wasn't going to get a shot at his big brother. My right hand found its anchor point at the corner of my mouth as the lead cow's head rose in surprise. Caribou were starting to scatter at the periphery of my vision. The bull I had my eye on hesitated and the shot felt perfect even before the release.

As my cedar arrow's yellow and white fletching disappeared into the bull's side, I knew that the long hunt was finally over.

Desperately Seeking Alaska

THERE ARE ONLY two kinds of serious bowhunters: those who have already hunted Alaska and those who hope to someday. Offering spectacular wilderness and a multitude of exotic species, Alaska is certainly the crown jewel of the North American outdoor experience, as earlier chapters of this book have hopefully demonstrated. Every year more bowhunters venture north to address this challenge. For some, the promise of a once-in-a-lifetime hunt is fulfilled, while others, unfortunately, go home disappointed.

Some of these disappointments are inevitable. If Alaska were as user friendly as California, twenty million people would live there. Wilderness is wilderness for a reason. Even though the last century has proven that Seward's original folly wasn't such a bad idea after all, Alaska still offers the continent's foulest weather, most rugged terrain, and a host of adversaries ranging in size from *Giardia* to grizzlies. No one ever said this was going to be easy.

Most disappointed visitors have no one to blame for their troubles but themselves. The most common mistake visiting bowhunters make is failing to appreciate how different Alaska is from anywhere else, even the wildest parts of the American west and Canada. With adequate preparation and respect for the unique demands of the north country, a self-guided bowhunt in the Great Land should be within reach of any reasonably experienced outdoorsman, but without such preparation even veterans can go astray.

One obvious solution to the logistical demands of an Alaskan hunt is to hire a qualified guide or outfitter. This approach will reduce the chances of a major breakdown in plans, but unless the nonresident hunter wants to pursue grizzlies, sheep, or, more recently, goats, a guide isn't legally necessary. Besides, I've found that the same personality traits that create bowhunters also make them place a premium on answering challenges on their own. So, with all due respect to my friends in the guiding and outfitting business, this chapter is not primarily addressed to their clients, but to the people who approach me every year and say: "I want to bowhunt Alaska. What should I do?"

Earlier chapters have, I hope, portrayed some of the enduring fascination of the north, the *why* of Alaska bowhunting if you will. While that is the aspect of the experience that interests me most as a writer, it wouldn't be right to avoid the *how* entirely. Here follow some practically oriented thoughts on bowhunting the Far North.

THE QUARRY

The first trip planning decision to make is simply a matter of deciding what species to pursue. Most newcomers to Alaska will probably select All of the Above. For a number of reasons, this understandably enthusiastic approach is neither realistic nor practical.

Alaska offers hunting for ten generally recognized big game species in addition to wolves and wolverines. (The number increases to eleven if you count brown and grizzly bears separately.) As noted, nonresident hunters need a licensed guide to hunt sheep, goats, and the big bears. Alaska offers excellent hunting for Sitka blacktailed deer, black bears, and, in limited areas, Roosevelt elk, but these species are available elsewhere. Most hunters traveling north have more exotic goals. Buffalo and musk oxen can be hunted only by special permits, which are difficult to obtain even for residents. That leaves moose and caribou as logical primary quarries for visitors planning unguided hunts.

There is a lot to be said for choosing the caribou. They are plentiful, widely distributed, and make a spectacular trophy. Alaska's caribou herds are in excellent biological condition. Seasons generally open in August, before most bow seasons in the lower forty-eight states. Because of their size, table quality, and their own unique trophy characteristics, moose are obviously an intriguing quarry as well. It should be noted that moose populations have not fared as well recently as the caribou have, and seasons are much more restricted. Since Alaskans love their annual freezer moose almost to the point of obsession, and there are almost no archery-only seasons in Alaska, one can expect rifle-toting company during moose season in all but the most inaccessible locations.

What about a multiple species hunt? Remember that Alaska is more of a subcontinent than a state, and despite the variety of game that lives there, these species don't necessarily inhabit the same places. Black bears and brown bears, for example, are almost mutually exclusive on the off-shore coastal islands. And while moose and blacktails both inhabit south-eastern Alaska, parasite problems limit their ability to cohabit.

Nonetheless, it can be done. Moose and caribou are a logical combination. They can be found together in many parts of the state, and seasons generally overlap for several weeks during September. A black bear can be added as an additional species almost anywhere in the state except the North Slope, and combination hunts for black bear and Sitka black-tails can be put together easily in the southeastern panhandle. With these exceptions, combination hunts will require special permits, guides, or separate trips to different parts of the state.

GETTING THERE

In the days of Teddy Roosevelt, Saxton Pope, and Art Young, just getting to Alaska was a major undertaking, and interested parties should read the chronicles of those early hunts for an appreciation of the area's original geographic isolation. The first part of the journey is far simpler now, since daily jet service can whisk the traveling outdoorsman into Anchorage, Fairbanks, or any of the larger communities in the southeastern panhandle. From there, most hunts involve scheduled air service to such traditional jumping off points as King Salmon, Iliamna, McGrath, or Bettles. Except for the scenery (weather permitting), this part of the trip isn't much different than flying to Chicago. All you need to get there is a travel agent and some money. From the touchdown of your last scheduled flight to the start of your bowhunt, however, matters get considerably more complicated. This is the most critical part of a self-guided hunt. Do it right and you will almost certainly have a positive experience no matter what you do or do not harvest in the field. Do it wrong and you may wish you never left home.

Visitors need to understand one principle at the outset. Bowhunting Alaska's limited road system for anything, with very few exceptions, is an exercise in futility. The ability to penetrate the wilderness away from roads and their attendant crowds is central to any successful hunt. Sometimes this can be accomplished by boat or horseback, and I have done my share of both, but the vast majority of successful Alaska bowhunters make the transition from civilization to hunting country by air. Like it or not, hunting Alaska means flying Alaska.

Aviation is so much a part of the Alaska outdoor experience that most residents, even nonpilots, know something about the basics of bush flying. Many visitors, on the other hand, have never even been inside a light aircraft before. Anyone planning a successful self-guided hunt in the Far North will have to acquire some familiarity with that venerable Alaska tradition, the bush air charter.

If you have nothing other than a general idea of where and what you want to hunt, you may wind up letting your air charter service do a lot of your trip planning for you. There is nothing wrong with this approach. As a rule, pilots know the areas they fly quite well, and even though they are not in the guiding business, they will usually be familiar with game populations and their access. Needless to say, some are better at this than others.

Begin by contacting several air charter services in the community from which you plan to depart. The Alaska Chamber of Commerce maintains a list of all such registered air charter services. While the Alaskan Bowhunter's Association is not in the business of endorsing specific commercial enterprises, there are quite a few air charter services on their list of sustaining members. These outfits have all demonstrated an interest in bowhunters, and this list is an excellent place to look for help. There is still no substitute for individual experience, and I would make every effort to contact personally someone who has flown the area before. Find out who they flew with and what they thought of the service. Research your final choice of air charter services as thoroughly as you would research the choice of a guide.

A few words of caution are in order before you turn your fate over blindly to an air charter service. Left to their own devices, most pilots will take their clients to locations that pose few technical problems for them. Unfortunately, these are areas that are likely to receive more than their share of pressure because of their very accessibility.

Ultimately, you will wind up with more satisfaction, solitude, and punched harvest tickets if you involve yourself more in the details of your trip planning. Begin with a careful review of the relevant topo maps and, if at all possible, obtain personal advice from someone who has hunted the area before. Develop several options. Just because you want to hunt one specific location doesn't mean there is any place to land an airplane. Sit down with your maps and your pilot and see what you can work out. Remember that the final decision about landing options is his and not yours. Do everyone a favor and don't try to insist on landing somewhere he doesn't want to land. Bush flying doesn't respond well to that kind of pressure. On the other hand, if he doesn't want to take you anywhere except the big blue lake in the middle of the map, it may be time for another opinion.

The next issue to confront is cost. There is no way around the fact that this will be the single most expensive part of the trip. Remember that the cost of operating commercial aircraft in Alaska is staggering. Everything from spare parts to liability insurance costs far more than it does anywhere else.

There are two basic ways charter operators bill for their time. Some simply charge a flat rate per hour of flight time, depending on the type of aircraft used. These rates generally don't vary much, at least within a given area. If you know exactly where you are going and how you want to get there, this may be the most economical approach. On the other hand, if you are not familiar with the area you may do better with a packaged fly out at a predetermined price. This figure should allow for scouting from the air, flying out meat, and even moving you to a different location if need be. While it may cost a little more per hour of air time, this system makes it easier to calculate costs in advance and may lead to a more productive hunt, especially if you don't have much Alaska experience under your belt.

Either way, remember that your air charter is the wrong place to look for a bargain on a long-awaited Alaska hunt. Cheap, packaged fly out hunts usually wind up in easily accessible areas close to population centers, and that is not what bowhunting Alaska is all about. The air charter business is highly competitive, and the successful ones stay in business by providing good service, not by cutting corners. After all the expense of buying nonresident tags and getting to Alaska, trying to compromise at this stage is false economy at its worst.

There are steps you can take to make sure you are getting the most for your money, however. The first is to be sure you are in the right kind of aircraft. Most Alaska bush flying is done in Super Cubs, high performance Cessnas, and the venerable DeHavilland Beaver. On the small end of the scale, Cubs offer many more landing options and cost less per hour of flight time, but carry far less useful load. Larger aircraft carry more gear, but cost more per hour to operate and require longer strips and lakes for landings and takeoffs. In general, you will do best from a financial standpoint flying in the smallest aircraft that can get you where you want to go in one trip. Landing options permitting, you will spend less money hauling yourself and your gear in one trip in a Beaver than in two trips in a 185. You may also be able to reduce costs by coordinating your trip with another party so that one of you can go out on the back haul from the other party's trip in.

The operation of the aircraft itself is strictly the pilot's responsibility, and you will do well to stay out of it for the most part. Two aspects of aircraft performance do concern you, however: weight and balance. All aircraft have a maximum weight at which they can operate safely. That weight will not change one bit because you really want to take an extra hundred pounds of equipment with you. When you have made a final decision about where you are going and what you will be flying in, ask your pilot for a maximum weight allowance and stick to it. How the load is distributed in the aircraft is also critical to flight performance. In general, light, bulky items like tents and sleeping bags can go to the rear, while heavy items need to be stowed closer to the aircraft's center of gravity. While it is the pilot's responsibility to worry about the details, you can help by showing up with your gear organized in lots of smaller bundles rather than fewer larger ones. Identify items that can tolerate a little moisture, since these can be carried in float compartments. If you have any long, awkward items, especially those that may need to be carried externally, let the pilot know well in advance.

A few final tips regarding your bush flight:

1. Ask your pilot to swing over your base camp if he is in the area. Arrange a simple signal system so that you can communicate from the ground. Space blankets work well for this purpose. Sample code: One blanket means land if you can. We have a moose to fly out. Two blankets means land! It's an emergency! There is actually a standard, complex system of signals for ground to air communication in a true emergency. No one can ever remember it, which is why (hint!) it is printed on the back of your Alaska hunting license.

2. Request a brief air tour of the area you plan to hunt. This will only add a few minutes of flight time to your bill and may be the best investment of the trip. Don't worry about spotting individual game animals. Focus instead on finding the best ways to get where you want to go on the ground.

3. Be sure someone at home knows where you are going, who you are flying with, and when you are expected back.

FOOD AND SHELTER

Because of the demands of Alaska's weather and terrain, a typical ten-day hunt can challenge the resources of even a seasoned woodsman. On a typical fly out hunt, you will be on your own from the time your pilot leaves you until you make contact again, a date that weather and other circumstances can delay considerably. Equipment failures and judgment errors may have consequences far beyond what they would elsewhere. You should be comfortable with basic wilderness survival skills before you set out; if you aren't, you owe it to yourself to hire a guide or talk a more experienced party into going with you. Even if you have spent time in the wild elsewhere, Alaska offers unique difficulties that you should be aware of before you depart.

On an Alaska hunt, a tent is more than a place to store equipment or duck into from an occasional rain shower. It is your final measure of security against serious weather and bugs. Your tent should be highly wind resistant, which many everyday tents are not. Domed designs and curved intrinsic frames fare better than traditional angular shapes when it really starts to blow, which it will if you stay out long enough. In the horizontal rain generated by typical Alaska fall storms, a stout rain fly is absolutely mandatory. Even the highest quality single-layer fabrics will leak under these conditions unless protected by a fly. At certain times of the year, bugproof mosquito netting is a necessity, not a luxury. Repellent and campfire smoke may make the bugs tolerable by day, but if they can get you at night you won't do much sleeping. Remember that if there is a hole in the netting, they will find it. Pitch your tent defensively, no matter how weatherproof you think it is. Exposed panoramas are great for glassing, but if a storm blows up you will wish you were in the trees. A needle, thread, and roll of duct tape should be available for emergency repairs.

Sleeping bags deserve an equal amount of care in their selection. As much as I appreciate down, the newer synthetics are generally superior in Alaska conditions because they retain so much more insulating capacity when they are wet. Damp sleeping bags are the rule rather than the exception no matter how carefully you camp. Don't scrimp on quality. Choose a bag comfort rated twenty degrees below the temperatures you expect to encounter. Sooner or later you will need the extra insulation.

On most camping trips, fires are a sort of social luxury, a means of making cold meals hot and a focus of activity after a hard day of hunting. In Alaska, they may mean much more. If you can build and maintain a fire, you can survive almost anything the elements throw at you. Fuel sources will often be wet, so practice your fire-starting skills in advance. I stuff small waterproof match containers everywhere. There is nothing like dropping your one box of matches in the river on the first morning of a ten-day float trip. As satisfying as it may be to coax a one-match fire to life from materials at hand, it is best to have the means to cheat available. Weight and space permitting, it never hurts to have a little extra white gas in camp.

If you will be camping above timberline, a lightweight backpack stove is a virtual necessity, and is hard to beat for convenience at any elevation. Stoves that burn butane canisters save the inconvenience of packing gasoline, but they perform poorly in cold weather. My Coleman Peak One® has warmed my meals more times than I can remember under all sorts of conditions, and it is a hard choice to beat for this sort of expedition.

The most important rule for the quartermaster on a wilderness hunt is simple: take enough food! Assume you will be weathered in for two or three extra days after your scheduled pickup date. That's about average, although delays will vary with the distance and terrain between your charter's base of operations and the hunt area. Take survival fare for an additional week. It doesn't have to be appetizing, but there should be plenty of it. Remember that you won't have to carry it any farther than the place you land. Fish and small game can often be used to supplement camp fare, but don't rely on them too heavily. Keep in mind that whenever you open a container, its contents become bear bait. Take lots of small cans so they can be burned clean and stored for packing out soon after using whatever is inside.

Aircraft weight considerations permitting, I think it is a good insurance policy to carry an extra package of essentials to base camp. On extended hunts, I usually bring an extra weatherproof duffel with a sleeping bag, small tent, freeze-dried food, and an extensive medical kit, and hang it in a bearproof cache before I start hiking. That way definitive survival gear is within reach in case of a true emergency.

CLOTHING AND PERSONAL GEAR

Moisture and rapidly fluctuating temperatures make it advisable to dress in layers on most Alaska hunts. Start with polypropylene or silk underwear to wick moisture away from the skin. The basis of my hunting clothing is always wool, which breathes well, is quiet, and retains significant insulating ability even when wet, which it usually is. Moisture is such a common problem that you won't see many experienced Alaska hunters wearing down except in the dead of winter. I usually carry a high quality Gore Tex® parka in my day pack, one that is light enough to carry without much inconvenience, but water resistant enough to keep me reasonably dry while hiking. I don't trust the stuff during extended periods of nasty weather, however, and like to carry a set of rubberized rain gear for camp use if possible.

When it comes to ruined trips, the Achilles heel for most Alaska hunters is, appropriately enough, the feet. The problem is simple to define. Whether hunting in lowland river bottoms or alpine tundra, your feel will almost always be on or in something wet. The result is, unfortunately, more serious than mere discomfort. Wet skin and long miles inevitably result in blisters, and blisters end hunts no matter how well motivated the hunter.

When hunting sheep or goats, I generally stick with well-conditioned leather boots, but at lower elevations pacs or hip waders are preferable. Most hip boots are designed for wading trout streams and not for hiking across country, but the ankle fit models are a tremendous improvement over the usual ponderous variety and are mandatory equipment for most moose, bear, and caribou hunts.

Leather boots will eventually soak through under typical Alaska hiking conditions no matter how well you treat them, while rubber boots will leave your feet damp because of internal condensation. Either way, you will have to act aggressively to prevent blisters. Start with lots of extra socks made from polypropylene, cotton, and wool. I carry extra pairs in my day pack and may change socks several times during the course of a long hike. Carry a good blister kit and use it at the first sign of trouble rather than waiting until skin is actually broken down. Tincture of benzoin, moleskin, and tape are the essentials, and they are available at any pharmacy.

Advice regarding archery tackle is simple: shoot what you shoot best. We all have a tendency to gear up for major trips. "Big hunt, big bow," the voice in the back of the brain tells us, but this is usually a mistake. Despite their size, moose and caribou are relatively easy to kill, and tackle adequate for black bears and elk is heavy enough to use on any game animal in Alaska. The often repeated claim that bowhunting Alaska means taking long shots makes my blood boil. Stalking in open terrain may present the *opportunity* to take longer shots than the whitetail hunter is accustomed to, but that doesn't mean he can or should take them. Know your effective range and stick to those distances; they aren't going to change just because you are in Alaska. If you are worried about your ability to manage under such conditions, I would suggest practicing your stalking skills rather than looking for some magical way to add to your effective range. The vast majority of my shots in Alaska have come under fifteen yards. That's the way you have to play the game if you aren't a particularly great shot, and I'm not. It also happens to be, in my opinion, just what the game is all about.

Once you have made it to the bush, you will have to be your own archery shop. Take two of everything you can't live without. Ptarmigan and grouse are often plentiful and provide a great means of keeping your shooting eye sharp. A brace of ptarmigan can also turn a pot full of noodles into a gourmet affair, so take lots of extra arrows.

Whether because of overenthusiasm, miscalculation, or success, you may wind up having to spend a night in the open. I've certainly done it more times than I care to remember, for all three reasons. If you are prepared, a siwash in the bush is nothing to be worried about, but if you aren't, your bowhunt may turn into a survival exercise. I find that I can always hunt more effectively if I'm not preoccupied with getting back to camp at night. I find it useful to carry a day pack with me at all times, and to have everything in that pack I need to hunt by day and stay out all night if need be. With good planning, the pack's weight can be kept to a minimum. That day pack is like a life vest to me, always either on my person or within arm's reach. If my raft swamps or my airplane winds up in the bushes, I know it will contain what I need to survive.

There are many variables beyond the hunter's control that can spell success or failure in the field, but one of the most important can be determined precisely: physical condition. Hunting Alaska is hard work, and to do it successfully and enjoyably, you need to be fit. Three months is the minimum lead time for a sedentary hunter to begin an exercise program prior to a strenuous hunt, and no one can do it for you.

HAZARDS OF THE NORTH

Alaska terrain is remarkably deceptive. A lot of it looks like easy going, but very little of it is. Lowland tundra is surprisingly difficult to hike across. Allow a lot more time than first seems necessary and stick to the high ground when feasible. Alders warrant special attention. Most of southcentral Alaska below three thousand feet of elevation supports dense alder growth on the steeper sidehills. Experienced hands soon learn to avoid these strips and patches of brush at almost any cost. Carrying a heavy backpack through dense alders is almost impossible. Study your route carefully before you start up or down hill and you should be able to thread your way around these impenetrable leads.

Statistically, the chance of a bad bear encounter should be near the bottom of anyone's list of worries. There is no doubt, however, that bears cause a lot of concern, and that concern has ample basis in fact. Every year there are a few serious bear maulings in Alaska and not always, as some would have you believe, because the victim did something foolish. Detailed advice for dealing with bears in the wild has been presented in an earlier chapter.

Jokes about Alaska's mosquitoes are common, famous, and often justified. Fortunately, hunting seasons generally occur after the bug season has peaked, but hunters should be prepared for mosquitoes and their equally obnoxious cousins, the white socks. A mosquito-proof tent is mandatory as is an ample supply of a DEET-containing repellent. I have seldom seen a situation during hunting season when I felt the need for a head net, but bugs don't bother me all that much. If you are sensitive to insect bites, you may wish to include one. White socks, which resemble the eastern black fly, can be hard on the hands, especially when trying to hold still. A pair of rubber surgical gloves is just the ticket under such circumstances and may spell the difference between a successful hunt and a spooked animal.

Less obvious than the mosquito, but just as capable of causing misery, *Giardia lamblia,* the parasite responsible for beaver fever, is a common inhabitant of Alaska's fresh water streams and lakes. When it sets up shop in your insides, as it will if you drink enough untreated water in the back country, you can expect an unpleasant bout of intestinal symptoms quite capable of ruining a hunt. It is wisest to assume that all fresh water is contaminated. Fortunately, boiling water even briefly ensures that it is no longer capable of transmitting giardiasis.

LEGAL CONSIDERATIONS

For administrative purposes, Alaska is divided into twenty-six Game Management Units. Many of them are larger than some eastern states, and with a dozen big game species to keep track of in addition to federally mandated and generally incomprehensible subsistence provisions, it is obvious that hunting regulations have to be extremely complex. Nonetheless, it is the hunter's responsibility to review the rules before the hunt and be familiar with all relevant regulations in the hunt area. Once in the bush, there won't be anyone else to ask, and ignorance doesn't carry much weight as an excuse with Fish and Wildlife Protection officers.

Some of the most common nonresident game citations occur because of failure to follow these regulations:

1. Once you have been airborne, you may not hunt until sunrise the following morning. (Exceptions: small game and Sitka blacktailed deer.)

2. All usable meat must be salvaged in the field. Think about this *before* you shoot a moose five miles from camp. (In the case of bears, salvaging the hide or the meat is acceptable.)

3. It is illegal to shoot a sow bear accompanied by cubs.

4. Nonresident hunters must be accompanied by a guide when hunting sheep, grizzly or brown bear, or goats.

Alaska law recognizes the demands that weather, wilderness, and unforeseen circumstances place on hunters in the bush. In the event of a legitimate emergency, one can violate virtually any game law for the sake of survival. The law does not require you to fight a brown bear for a hindquarter of moose and it makes allowance for unanticipated weather that may result in spoiled meat or the need to shoot a game animal out of season in order to survive. But should you invoke such emergency provisions, you had better be able to prove your case. Alaska's game wardens are dedicated professionals. They have all heard their share of war stories over the years and know full well that Alaska's wild heritage depends on them to separate fact from fiction.

THE MYSTIQUE OF THE NORTH

Bowhunting Alaska is not necessarily an ordeal. It is a challenge, and can *become* an ordeal, but with proper planning and preparation a self-guided hunt should be within the capabilities of any well-motivated, physically fit bowhunter.

The key element of a successful Far North hunt may have less to do with any of the details than it does with attitude. Alaska hunts are expensive, rigorous, and time consuming. If you assume that the north owes you a trophy in return for your investment, you may well return home disappointed. On the other hand, if you make Alaska itself your objective and go there to see new sights, meet new people, study exotic wildlife, and rise to the challenge of the last true wilderness on the continent, you will almost certainly succeed. Treat that set of trophy antlers as the bonus it really is, and you may be surprised to find how justly it comes your way.

SIXTEEN

Ashes to Ashes

A FOUR-YEAR-OLD-BOAR, he wasn't particularly large even by the less than large standards of interior Alaska black bears, yet he will always be a trophy to me. He was eight feet away from me on the open tundra when I finally shot him. The cedar arrow whistled through his rib cage without even stopping. After the shot, the bear loped fifty yards downhill and collapsed at the base of an alder patch in a wet black heap, and that was all.

After circling the bear carefully to confirm that he was as dead as he looked, I hauled him away from the edge of the brush. It had been raining all week and the lichen underfoot was squishy and as slick as spilled oil. Camp lay four miles away, and less than two hours of light remained in the gray sky overhead before nightfall.

I snapped a few hurried photographs and began to skin the bear. He was plump after a late summer orgy of fish and berries, and my fingers slid awkwardly along the greasy edge of the rich black fur as I worked. The knife blade was an accident waiting to happen. When the hide finally fell free from the carcass, I cut out the back straps, boned the hams, rolled the meat inside the skin, and dumped the whole oleaginous mess into my backpack, which for some reason I had the foresight to carry with me that afternoon.

On the ridge behind me, the ceiling was coming down fast. Even though I was familiar with the terrain, I took a compass bearing toward the distant river bend where the security of camp lay waiting. Underneath my rain gear, woolen clothes lay wet and heavy against my skin. I could no longer remember what it was like to be warm and dry. Once I was certain where I was going and how I was going to get there, I grunted my way into the pack straps, picked up my longbow, and began the long slide down off the mountain.

The next morning, the river finally spilled over its banks. The rafting there is not difficult under ordinary conditions, but now great surges of wild current drove us across the willow bars, and we shared the river with logs and stumps and other floating debris. When we finally drifted into the herds of migrating caribou that we had been looking for all week, there was nothing to do but admire them as they milled around us on the flooded banks. There were miles to go before the river opened up enough to accommodate a float plane, and the last thing we needed to deal with under these circumstances was a dead caribou.

Each night, after we secured the rafts against the flood and made what camp we could on the highest ground available, I took the bear hide out of the pack and tried to let it breathe. Salting it was impossible. Despite the grim outlook for its preservation, I kept it close at hand as we drifted on down the river and continued to nurture it like a child, for reasons that anyone who has stalked within eight feet of a bear on open ground and killed it cleanly with an arrow can understand.

Three days after the kill, the Beaver step-taxied across the lake's smooth surface on the last leg of the long journey home. I realized that the sense of arrival that flavors the return from even the most routine trips into the bush seemed strangely lacking. My inner compass had lost its bearings. I was in the process of leaving Alaska and moving back to Montana. During my absence on the hunt, my wife had left to drive our horses and the last of our household possessions down the highway. Our house was gone, sold and now occupied by its new owners. I had less than a week to conclude my affairs and head south myself. I realized wistfully that the bear hide in the pack under my feet represented the last game animal I was going to harvest as an Alaska resident. A chapter of my life was over, and it seemed that I might never truly feel young again.

On the way to my friend Joe Kelly's house, where I planned to spend the next few hectic days, I stopped and bought ten pounds of salt. Even before I unpacked my gear and my mildewed clothing, I spread the bear hide on his basement floor where I finished fleshing it, split the lips, turned the ears, and salted everything completely. When I submerged myself at last in a steaming bath, I began to believe that I might actually have salvaged the bear hide after all.

When Sheli picked me up at the Billings airport five days later, my worldly goods consisted of my backpack, a tubular case containing my bow and a half-dozen arrows, and a duffel bag with the salted bear hide inside. Sheli and I embraced enthusiastically without regard for the other passengers at the boarding gate, who no doubt felt that we were a little too old for that kind of thing. It didn't matter to us. I told her about the bear and the flood on the river. She told me about the long trip down the highway with the horses behind her in the trailer and winter closing in from all sides, and I realized just how glad I was to see her all over again. As we pulled away from the airport and began the long drive home across the prairie, it occurred to me that the only fixed points of reference during this period of upheaval were my family, my bow, and the bear hide resting in the back of the truck.

The following morning, I paid a visit to an old friend. Although I hadn't seen him for over six years, I still regarded him as my taxidermist. He is a quiet man and I know little of his personal values, but he understands the nuances of his craft better than anyone I know. For all practical purposes, he is an artist.

I make no apology for my fascination with the heads and horns of game animals. This regard has nothing to do with record books, in which I have no interest. There is something primal in their appeal, and I can take the analysis no further than that. Usually I am content to saw a skull in two, bleach the bone, and nail the result to my wall somewhere like the subject of a Georgia O'Keefe painting. Sometimes, however, more is called for, and when it is, I take whatever I've got to my taxidermist: a Dall ram that is no more than a representative of the species to anyone but me, an atypical mule deer that is exceptional for this part of Montana, a barren ground caribou that would be exceptional by any standard. He preserved them all for me, and in doing so preserved as well the memory of their taking and the fine, wild places in which I took them. When visitors comment on the presence of animal heads and antlers in every corner of the house, I seldom bother to reply. They either understand or they don't.

And now, all I asked of my taxidermist was that he do all this again for the bear I had taken at a range so close that shooting him seemed like awakening from a dream.

My taxidermist's skill with eyes and ears does not extend to public relations. His usual response to whatever I have brought him is to observe that a fella could mount one like that if he had a mind to. I have heard him make such comments about some fairly impressive animals. What he says to out-of-staters who bring in three-point mule deer and immature antelope, I cannot begin to imagine.

During my first season in that area, years before my Alaska interlude, Ray Stalmaster downed an immense cock sage hen that was neither shot up nor mauled by our young, undisciplined retrievers. He wrapped the bird delicately in his game vest and carried it from the field. The specimen arrived at the taxidermist's shop in beautiful condition. "A fella could mount that one," he observed after a critical inspection. "Course you're going to shoot lots of bigger ones." Chastened, we drove home and turned the sage hen into spaghetti sauce or some damn thing despite the fact that neither of us had ever seen one nearly so large. Fifteen years later, we still haven't.

And so I didn't expect effusive praise as I rolled the bear hide out on the floor and told him briefly of its epic journey from the Alaska wilderness to his shop. He poked and prodded for a minute or so and finally declared that the hide was in acceptable condition. "Course you got yourself some extra holes here and there," he observed. I started to tell him about the rain and the cold and my numb, helpless fingers and the overwhelming loneliness I felt as I skinned the bear, but thought better of it.

"Hair ain't half bad," he noted as he straightened from the floor. "You want an open mouth rug?"

"Sure," I said, although I hadn't really given it much thought.

"You'll get tired of looking at it," he said with disapproval.

"To tell you the truth," I said as all the tensions of the last disjointed month came welling up inside me, "I don't know what I want. He can have his mouth open. He can have his mouth closed. He can be picking his damn nose for all I care. I just want the hide tanned so it won't rot and I can stop worrying about it."

My taxidermist must have sensed an impending psychotic break. "A fella could sure do that," he reassured me. "We'll just get it tanned and figure the rest of it out later."

That sounded fine to me.

I picked up the tanned hide the following spring. It looked good and it felt good. There were indeed a few extra holes, the legacy of my desperate skinning technique in the face of the cold and the rain, but when I saw the light shining through them I remembered the urgency of the work there on the wet tundra and the long hike back down the mountain in the dark, and they didn't bother me at all. My taxidermist assured me they could be repaired easily when it came time to mount the hide. He told me to take the bear skin home, roll it up like a sleeping bag, and store it in the freezer until I made a final decision about what I wanted to do with it. The plan seemed simple enough to me.

Three years later, the hide still hadn't really found a home. The coat was uniform and unrubbed as one would expect on a fall bear, and since it looked too good to consign to the freezer, I simply draped it over the banister that flanks my stairwell. The kids always stroked it gently as they passed, and my old Labrador growled at it suspiciously right up until the day he died. The hide looked a little tattered in its unfinished state, but I could look at it lying there and remember the sound the broadhead made when it disappeared into the bear.

Then one summer afternoon, I studied a blank spot on the living room wall between the mule deer and some moose horns and decided that this would be an ideal place for a head and shoulder mount of the bear. I gathered the hide from the railing where it had lain informally in state for so long and drove to my taxidermist's shop. I explained what I wanted and as expected he allowed that a fella could indeed do such a thing if he had a mind to. I left feeling that the bear, like some disturbed spirit, was at last on its way to a final resting place.

Bow season lasts three full months in Montana, and during that time I forgot all about the bear, just as I forget about a lot of other mundane things when the elk are talking and the whitetails are laying down scrapes. It has been that way for so long that I don't worry about it any-more, and neither does anyone else who knows me.

By December, there was nothing left to hunt but lions. One morn-ing when the tracking snow had melted, I finally remembered the bear. Because there was nothing else to do, I drove down to my taxidermist's shop to see how things were going.

I walked through the door without knocking, as I always do. A wood stove glowed in the corner of the shop. A half-dozen nearly com-pleted heads lined the walls: a well-haired goat, an average antelope, a more than respectable whitetail. I cannot remember the rest. There was no bear. My taxidermist was tuning a guitar in the next room. I made some throat-clearing noises, and he put the instrument down and joined me.

"Making any progress with that bear?" I asked.

"Yeah," he said, "but it's all bad."

Suddenly, I was confused and apprehensive, as when you encounter an unfavorable sign on a blood trail. This couldn't be right, I told myself. I had already shot this one.

"Did you store that hide in the freezer?" he asked.

I admitted that I had not.

"Here's what happened," he explained. "I cut the front part of the hide off and soaked it so I could work it onto the form. It just fell apart.

I'll let you see for yourself." He disappeared into a back room and re-turned moments later with a box full of black fur. I ran my fingers briefly through the fragments. It still felt thick and rich, but it was no longer part of anything.

"I should have asked you if you'd kept it in the freezer," he said. "That keeps them from falling apart when you soak them."

"It's not your fault," I assured him. "You told me what to do and I didn't do it."

"I'm still sorry," he said. "I know how hard you bowhunters work at this." I could tell that he meant it. There wasn't anything more to say.

I carried the box containing what was left of the hide back out to the truck as if it were a casket. A front was approaching and it had started to snow. Thick, wet flakes fell heavily against the open box. Still warm from the shop, the black fur caught the fallen flakes and held them briefly before they melted. I set the box in the back of the pickup and watched the snow fall on it and disappear. I remembered the rain on the distant mountain and the raw pelt's greasy feel between my fingers and the yearning desire to embrace Alaska—tantalizing, elusive Alaska—one last time before I left. Those were the qualities of the north's character that made me treasure the bear, and those were the same qualities that made me unable to possess it.

By the time I started the truck and left for home, the wet, white glop falling from the sky had started to look like tracking snow again.